— THE BIG BOOK OF —
CROSS STITCH
FABULOUS PROJECTS AND CREATIVE IDEAS

THE BIG BOOK OF
CROSS STITCH
FABULOUS PROJECTS AND CREATIVE IDEAS

JAN EATON AND DOROTHEA HALL

NEW
HOLLAND

First published in the UK in 2002 by
New Holland Publishers (UK) Ltd
Garfield House, 86-88 Edgware Road
London W2 2EA
www.newhollandpublishers.com
London • Cape Town • Sydney • Auckland

2 4 6 8 10 9 7 5 3

ISBN 1 84330 105 9 (pbk)

Designer: Ian Sandom
Production: Hazel Kirkman
Editorial Co-ordinator: Emily Preece-Morrison
Editors: Jo Finnis, Felicity Jackson, Elizabeth Rowe, Emma Callery
Photographers: Steve Tanner, Jon Stewart
Charts and illustrations: John Hutchinson, Geoff Denney, Andy Waterman,
Jo Finnis, Chris Mullen, Julie Ward, King and King, Simone End,
Debra Woodward, Sarah Willis, Lizzie Saunders, Claire Davies
Stylist: Barbara Stewart

Reproduction by Modern Age Repro House Ltd, Hong Kong
Printed and bound in Malaysia by Times Offset (M) Sdn. Bhd.

The right of the authors to be identified has been asserted
in accordance with the Copyright, Designs and Patents Act 1988.

Acknowledgements

The authors would like to thank the following: DMC for supplying embroidery fabrics,
threads and needlework accessories; Cara Ackerman of DMC Creative World;
Wendy Bailey; Nigel Benson of 20th Century Glass; Charlotte Parry-Crooke;
Clare Royals; Gillie Spargo, John Goodall.

CONTENTS

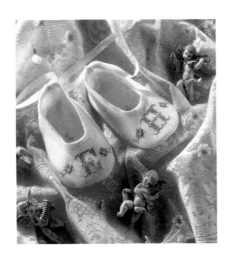

HISTORY AND DEVELOPMENT

The first stitches were used to join animal skins to make clothing. The first textiles were probably crudely constructed from grass and other plant materials, until a way was found to twist fibres and animal hairs into continuous strands by spinning. From about 10,000 BC until the development of synthetic fibres in the twentieth century, the raw materials for textiles came from four natural fibres: wool and silk from the animal world and cotton and flax from plants.

Embroidery probably began as a means of strengthening a fabric by darning in extra threads, then developed gradually into the decorative process we know today. Fragments of cloth dating from between 5000 BC and 500 AD have been excavated in South and Central America, Egypt and China, and these show crude examples of darning, half cross stitch and satin stitch. Many of the fragments are linen; the regular weave of this fabric, one of the oldest of woven materials, provided the basis for the development of counted thread stitches. Over many centuries embroidery has been practised by both rich and poor, amateur and professional, and used to personalize household linen and possessions; to enrich domestic and ecclesiastical garments and accessories; to decorate furnishings and add ornament to ceremonial robes and banners.

THE ORIGINS OF CROSS STITCH

The earliest example of cross stitch is thought to date from about 500 AD. The design is worked completely in upright crosses on linen, and the fragment was discovered in a Coptic cemetery in Upper Egypt. Very few pieces of decorated fabric have survived from ancient and early Christian civilisation, but this does not necessarily mean that decorative stitching was rarely used. Natural fabrics are perishable and do not survive as well as the many metal and ceramic artefacts found in archaeological sites.

There is not yet sufficient evidence available to enable us to trace the exact origins of cross stitch embroidery. Some historians suggest that the development of cross stitch owes much to the craftsmanship of the Chinese, since cross stitch embroidery is known to have flourished during the T'ang Dynasty between 618 AD and 906 AD. It is quite feasible that these cross stitch designs and techniques subsequently spread from China via India and Egypt to the civilisations of Greece and Rome, and from there throughout the countries of the eastern Mediterranean and the Middle East. An alternative school of thought suggests that the spread of cross stitch embroidery may have been in entirely the opposite direction, since the first important migration of foreign people into China took place during the T'ang Dynasty. Persians, Arabs and travellers from Greece and India followed

LEFT: Early samplers were used by needlewomen to experiment with stitches, techniques and designs. They later became exercises in education, giving children practice in spelling and stitching skills.

RIGHT: This collection of cross stitch embroideries and pieces of decorated china incorporates design motifs from around the world, which illustrates that the possibilities of this form of counted thread embroidery are almost limitless.

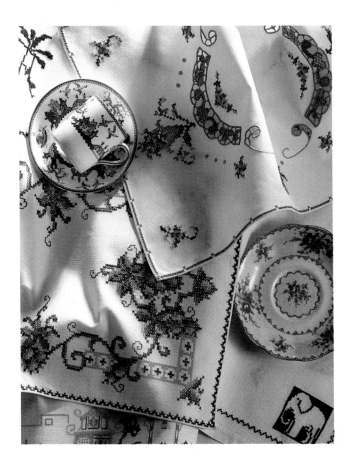

the silk routes to China and many eventually settled there. There is some evidence to suggest that these immigrants influenced the designs used in Chinese arts and crafts, particularly those for textiles. Many Chinese textiles bear motifs that show great similarity to those found on Persian fabrics.

What is certain, however, is that the techniques and designs of cross stitch spread from many of these countries throughout the European continent. The Crusaders probably brought home embroidered textiles from the Middle Eastern countries after the Crusades, and the trade and spice routes carried not only articles for sale but also itinerant craftsmen, who practised their skills wherever they settled. The spread of cross stitch designs from their place of origin to so many different locations makes it difficult to identify any one cross stitch design as having originated in any particular region. Even today, it is fascinating to note the same motifs occurring in the traditional peasant embroideries of countries as far apart, geographically, as Russia and Mexico.

THE ENGLISH TRADITION

The earliest reference to embroidery in England occurs in a document dating from 679 AD. During the following centuries, embroidery enriched ceremonial vestments belonging both to Church and royalty, and it is probable that domestic versions existed but have not survived. There is, however, little evidence in Europe of the use of cross stitch or its variations before the sixteenth century, with the exception of the badge of the Knight's Templar on the Syon Cope, now exhibited at the Victoria and Albert Museum, London. Crossed stitches began to be commonly used during the sixteenth century, worked on needlepoint hangings, table covers, carpets and furniture coverings by the female households of the courts and castles.

During this period, embroidery was worked either in home-produced woollen threads or silk imported from the Middle East. A linen fabric known as 'canvas' was used as the background and cross stitch was often worked together with tent stitch and satin stitch. Some stitches, such as the double running or Holbein stitch used to outline cross stitch areas, are thought to have been introduced to England by Catherine of Aragon, the first wife of Henry VIII. Embroidery designs were copied from a number of sources, including woven tapestry hangings, herbals and gardening

books. Jacques Le Moyne's *La Clef des Champs*, published in 1586, is often quoted as an influential design source. Many examples of fine stitching were recorded in the contemporary portraits of that period.

Throughout the sixteenth century, furniture was heavy and rather uncomfortable, and padded cushions helped to provide welcome comfort and warmth in the home. Inventories throughout this period show that embroidered cushions were used in both great and humble houses. An inventory drawn up in 1523 lists cushions covered with 'velvet of divers colours imbrodered with golde' and 'tawny sarcenet imbrodered with branchis'.

Sixteenth century embroiderers stitched emblematic designs in addition to the stylized floral patterns from the design books. These abstract motifs were usually copied from pieces of embroidered fabric which had been brought into England from other parts of Europe, or from further afield. Queen Elizabeth I was reputedly a fine needlewoman, as was Mary Queen of Scots who filled the months of her captivity producing exquisite examples of embroidery, often using cross stitch, some of which survive today.

After the restoration of the monarchy in 1660, domestic life in Britain became more comfortable. Women embroidered many more decorative items than before, including pictures and firescreens which often featured realistic biblical scenes. As travel and trade increased, voyagers returned from the Far East and the Americas bringing new design sources which could be utilized. Strange foreign flowers, beasts and birds found their way into traditional embroidery patterns. When adapted for cross stitch, the designs often lost much of their original form and became merely decorative details.

By the middle of the eighteenth century, many of the great houses of the land had 'needlework rooms' where large panels of needlepoint and tapestry were mounted on the walls, framed by elaborately carved mouldings. However, after that time the popularity of embroidery and needlepoint seems to have declined a little, probably due to changes of fashion in home furnishings. When printed fabrics became available in large quantities, people were provided with a cheap alternative to heavy tapestries and needlepoint panels.

The British middle classes were beginning to enjoy increasing wealth during the early part of the nineteenth century. This prosperity was mainly due to large profits from industrialization, and the middle classes soon began to share the leisure pursuits which had previously been the prerogative of the upper classes. From the 1850s onwards, most middle class women and young girls spent a great deal of time doing embroidery and 'fancy work' (crafts like crochet, tatting and macrame). Their houses were full of decorated cushions, mats, pictures, antimacassars, doilies, and other articles worked from patterns in the growing number of weekly women's magazines. These items were generally displayed in the main rooms, purely as decoration and as a way of showing off the skills of the ladies of the house. Cross stitch was still used, but mainly for sampler stitching until interest in a type of cross stitch embroidery known as 'Berlin woolwork' spread throughout Europe and America.

SAMPLERS

Personal collections of stitches and designs have been embroidered for hundreds of years by both women and children. These collections are called samplers (from the Old French 'essamplaire', meaning a pattern which could be copied) and many have survived to the present day, forming a unique record of domestic needlework from the fifteenth to the twentieth century. Samplers were worked primarily as a learning process to try out different stitches, techniques and designs which could then be used as reference material. The designs were probably copied by one person and then passed on to someone else, so many of the samplers show similar designs worked in different ways. The earliest reference occurs in 1502, when the account book of Elizabeth of York showed the purchase of 'lynnyn cloth for a sampler'.

Early samplers show realistic and fanciful flowers, fruit, animals, birds and figures as well as border patterns, and many of the designs were copied from printed pattern books. The samplers were worked on linen fabric or fine canvas using silk, linen or wool threads and used a variety of stitches and techniques including cross stitch, cut and drawn thread work and metal thread embroidery. Later samplers, particularly those from the eighteenth and nineteenth centuries, are worked mainly in cross stitch and show an increasing use of alphabets and religious texts.

During the nineteenth century, the majority of samplers were stitched by children in schools and orphanages as part of their general education. Embroidered samplers were based on the alphabet to give pupils a thorough grounding in the sequence of letters, spelling and also in practical embroidery skills. After leaving school, many girls went into domestic service. Having a good standard of spelling and needlework meant that they could hope to avoid menial kitchen work and perhaps become a lady's maid. A lady's maid would spend much of her time repairing garments and marking the household linen with embroidered names and monograms, so neat stitching and accurate spelling was essential.

Girls usually worked one complete alphabet sampler each year during their schooldays and, in most schools, the teacher also kept a needlework exercise book and carefully recorded the progress of her pupils. Many of these books have survived intact and show examples of each child's work stitched or pinned to the pages. In addition to embroidery, small samples of knitting, crochet, patchwork and plain sewing were included. A typical book of this kind was worked by pupils of the Westbourne Union School, Sussex during the period 1842 to 1844. Each page of work is headed by a strip of canvas showing the girl's name and age worked in cross stitch.

Most nineteenth century samplers contain one or two simple alphabets and sets of numerals enclosed within a narrow border. The stitches are usually worked in coloured cross stitch on coarse woollen fabric or occasionally on linen. Ordinary cross stitch and marking cross stitch are usually the only stitches used on this type of sampler. The date of completion and the Christian name and surname of the stitcher and her age were usually added. Complex monochrome samplers were also produced, usually by girls living in orphanages, some containing as many as twenty alphabets, moral verses, religious texts and motifs of houses, animals and flowers.

RIGHT: Cross stitch embroidery is a perennially popular way of decorating items of household linen. During the 1920s and '30s, transfer-printed designs were widely available, often in kit form.

Sampler texts tended to be sombre and worthy. A sampler completed in 1883 shows a tiny bible surrounded by the words 'Behold the BOOK whose leaves display JESUS the life the truth the way'. Inscriptions on other samplers include 'God is love abide with us time is short' and 'Remember thy Father and Mother in the days of thy youth'. On some samplers, the wording is a little more human - one mid-Victorian example reveals 'here a figure there a letter one done bad another better'.

As well as embroidery, plain sewing was taught in schools. An educational manual, *Plain needlework in all its branches*, published in 1849 for use in the National Industrial School of the Holy Trinity at Finchley, London, states the need for all women to have 'a practical acquaintance with needlework ... this is more particularly the case with reference to females in humble life, whether with a view to domestic neatness and economy, or to profitable occupation in a pecuniary light'. The manual lists twelve basic stitches including cross stitch, buttonhole stitch and herringbone stitch. Sewing samplers were worked on white linen or cotton and illustrate the range of techniques used to create the garments and household linen of the day. The fabric was first hemmed, then cut and darned. Buttonholes, covered buttons, hooks, eyes and fabric tags and tapes were added as well as types of seams and shaping techniques, such as tucks and gathers. These samplers often show exquisite workmanship and many include decorative stitching, such as names and dates, worked in cross stitch or chain stitch.

BERLIN WOOLWORK

Berlin woolwork was a type of cross stitch embroidery which first appeared in Berlin during the 1830s. It was worked on canvas using a great variety of different coloured woollen threads. The designs were printed in chart form on squared paper, with one square representing one stitch. By counting the squares and stitching them with the correct shades of thread, the needle-women could copy the designs accurately. Berlin woolwork was used extensively for pictures and to cover cushions, chair seats and stools as well as to make small items like slippers, pincushions and purses. Three-dimensional areas were produced by the use of a textured stitch called velvet stitch. Portions of the design were closely worked in this stitch and the resulting pile trimmed with scissors to give an almost sculptured effect. The charts were originally printed in black line on white paper and laboriously hand coloured, but as the craze swept through Europe and America, later charts were printed in full colour to keep up with the demand.

Special woollen threads were spun for woolwork and these took a faster, more brilliant dye than the worsted threads which had previously been used for embroidery. The threads were manufactured at Gotha in Germany and dyed in Berlin. They had a soft, silky finish and were called 'Berlin wool' or 'Zephyr yarn'. With the introduction of aniline dyes in the 1850s, the colours became more brilliant and rather gaudy. Berlin woolwork was usually worked on white cotton 'German' canvas, as this was extremely hardwearing and every tenth thread was coloured yellow to aid counting.

Floral designs were particularly popular for woolwork articles. Floral garlands and bouquets were usually worked against a light-coloured background. Early designs of passion flowers, roses, pansies, auriculas and other small blooms look delicate and almost lifelike but, by about 1860, exotic flowering plants like fuchsias, arum lilies and hothouse orchids were used in profusion, usually worked on a black background.

As the craze for Berlin woolwork increased, the designs became more florid and crude, and the embroidered results looked garish. Extremely bright colours were used for the designs, with detailed, naturalistic shading on the petals and leaves. Other favourite subjects of the period were birds and animals, particularly parrots and macaws. Copies of sentimental paintings by some of the eminent artists of the day, including Sir Edwin Landseer, were also popular subjects. In America, there was a craze for portraiture worked in Berlin woolwork, particularly depicting George Washington and Benjamin Franklin, whose features graced cushion covers and pictures by the thousand. Highlights of silk thread and glass beads were often added to the portraits, creating the effect of light and shade.

During the 1860s and 1870s, naturalistic designs gradually declined in popularity and were replaced by ornamental and geometric patterns, such as Greek key borders, scrolls and arabesques. The women's magazines of the period reflected this trend and *The Young Ladies' Journal* of 1864 contained many charts for geometric borders. The magazine's editorial states that 'We continue to supply our readers with as many designs in strips and borders in Berlin work as possible because we are assured of their utility. It is quite easy to be working these strips ... when worked they may be used for so many purposes - cushions, stools, borders of table-covers and travelling bags, etc.'

RIGHT: Cross stitch is found on traditional embroideries in many diverse cultures throughout the world. In these examples from Thailand, cross stitch is worked alongside satin stitch and hand appliqué.

THE LAST HUNDRED YEARS

By the mid 1880s, the popularity of Berlin woolwork was declining, both in Europe and America. Gradually the florid, brightly-coloured woolwork designs began to be replaced by designs based on the study of ancient and ethnic textiles. The Royal School of Needlework was founded in London in 1872, with the twin aims of improving the general standard of embroidery and design and also to provide employment for women with needlecraft skills. The commissions undertaken by these women showed a high standard of technical excellence, and the results were especially pleasing when the designs were the work of leading artists and illustrators of the period, such as William Morris and Walter Crane. The RSN gave classes in embroidery techniques and the ladies in their workshops repaired and restored old textile pieces of value and special interest.

In 1876, the RSN exhibited some of its specially commissioned 'art needlework' at the Centennial Exposition in Philadelphia. The innovative designs and technical skill of these exhibits was influential in reviving interest in

embroidery. Candace Wheeler, an American fabric designer, and Louis Tiffany, a leader of the American Art Nouveau movement, founded the Society for Decorative Arts in New York, which helped raise and revitalize the standards of American design and craftsmanship in a wide range of crafts.

The study of old embroideries has uncovered a rich source of embroidery stitches and designs. As transport to foreign countries became safer, more comfortable and less expensive, more women began to travel abroad. They often brought back pieces of folk art embroidery, especially from Eastern Europe, Italy, India and the Aegean, which they studied and eventually copied. In 1920, the Embroiderers' Guild was formed and its first president, Louisa Pesel, did much to popularize traditional embroidery stitches such as cross stitch, pattern darning and double running stitch. Miss Pesel encouraged Guild members to take an active interest in using traditional designs and motifs from both historical and ethnic sources. Her research amongst the textiles in museum and private collections brought to light a wide range of lovely and forgotten cross stitch designs. Many of these were published in book form during the 1930s and are still in use today.

Hand embroidery remained a popular pursuit for many women throughout the first half of the twentieth century, together with crochet and hand knitting, and enjoyably filled many hours of spare time at home before the age of television. Many of the attractive pictures and pieces of table linen which survive from the twenties and thirties were probably bought in kit form from catalogues and draper's shops. The kits contained linen or cotton fabric printed with a design ready to be stitched using the supplied threads. Cross stitch designs of the period varied from multi-coloured, naturalistic patterns and folk art borders, through to abstract designs showing a strong Art Deco influence. Transfers for cross stitch could be bought without fabric and threads, or were given away free with the popular women's magazines of the day to boost their circulation. The design was printed on the transfer paper with a waxy ink, and was transferred to the fabric at home by pressing the wrong side of the transfer with a hot iron. The most elaborate pieces were much prized, often remaining unused for several generations, and have become treasured articles passed down through the family from mother to daughters, taking on the status of family heirlooms.

Interior design styles changed radically during the post-war years and there was no place for old-fashioned, elaborately embroidered home furnishings. The restrained Scandinavian styles of embroidery, such as Hardanger work and geometric designs in cross stitch, were much in demand during this period.

The late sixties and early seventies heralded a growing awareness of natural and ethnic designs, and this was reflected in both interior decoration and fashion. Inexpensive foreign holidays encouraged more people to travel abroad and many of them brought back garments and furnishings decorated with peasant embroidery. Today, with leisure time increasing, more and more men and women have begun to enjoy the craft and skills of cross stitch embroidery.

CROSS STITCH ROUND THE WORLD

Cross stitch has been used to decorate fabric in almost every part of the world, from Eastern Europe to Thailand; from Russia to Morocco. Designs and stitches have been exchanged between so many different cultures and geographical areas, through travel, trade and the availability of printed design books, that many design elements are now common to several cultures. However, there are many regional variations of similar cross stitch shapes, for example star, heart, flower and animal motifs.

One of the most important and widespread functions of cross stitch has been to ornament peasant garments and household linens, often as a means of indicating family wealth and status. Peasant embroidery is a purely domestic skill which is passed down through the generations from mother to daughter. The stitches are simple to work and the materials readily available. The thread colours were often limited, although these would be brilliantly dyed, often with the addition of brown or black for outlines. In China, cross stitch was almost always worked in dark blue thread on white fabric. Embroideries stitched in just one or two colours are perhaps the most striking of all and show off a complicated design to best advantage.

Complex and closely worked border patterns were actually created in the simplest way. Motifs used on their own are uncommon in peasant embroidery; instead they are usually repeated to form straight bands, which are then arranged one above another. Traditional Greek designs have as many as six or seven put together to form an intricate border, which is usually finished with a pattern that creates a broken outer edge.

RIGHT: Cross stitch designs from India are usually spaced by eye, rather than by counting fabric threads. The colours and designs are delightfully exuberant, reflecting both Eastern and Western influences.

CROSS STITCH
FOR THE HOME

MID PLEASURES AND PALACES THOUGH
WE MAY ROAM,
BE IT EVER SO HUMBLE, THERE'S NO PLACE
LIKE HOME.

Clari, the Maid of Milan
H PAYNE

APPLE BLOSSOM TEACLOTH

*Delicately shaded sprays of apple blossom linked by sections of striped ribbon border make
this cloth the perfect background for an afternoon meal of delicious cakes and refreshing tea.*

MATERIALS

- 130 cm (51 in) by 130 cm (51 in) wide 18 count
  white Aida evenweave fabric
- DMC stranded cotton: see the thread list below
- Tapestry needle size 24
- Tacking thread in a dark colour
- Matching sewing thread
- Sewing needle and pins
- Large embroidery hoop

THREAD LIST

3731	mid dusty pink	740	bright orange
3733	dusty pink	700	bright green
62	light shaded pink	704	light green
112	mid shaded pink	890	very dark green
304	dark red	954	pastel green

*BELOW: Embroider this charming, old-fashioned border round the
edge of your cloth, or just use the corner motifs for a simpler effect.*

WORKING THE EMBROIDERY

1 Tack a vertical line through the centre of the fabric, taking care not to cross any vertical threads. Mark the central horizontal line in the same way. Along one side of the fabric, tack a guideline 32 cm (12½ in) from the edge.

2 Begin at the centre of this side, noting that the tacked line gives the position of the centre of each flower motif. Mount the fabric in the embroidery hoop (page 132) and work one border flower motif in cross stitch (page 134) from the chart, using four strands of thread in the needle throughout. Start stitching at the centre of the orange area and work outwards, remembering that each square on the chart represents one cross stitch worked over three vertical and three horizontal woven blocks of fabric. Use a mixture of shaded pinks (62 and 112) for the petals. Outline the petals in dark red (304) and add leaf veins in very dark green (890) in back stitch (page 134) using two strands of thread in the needle.

3 Working towards one corner of the fabric from the completed flower motif, embroider two repeats of the ribbon border in the same way, then embroider the corner flower motif. At this point, stop and check your embroidery thoroughly, making sure that the motifs are complete and that the centre of each flower falls along the tacked line.

4 Tack a guideline from the centre of the completed corner flower motif along the adjacent side of the fabric towards the second corner. Work two repeats of the pink ribbon border and one border flower motif along this side. Work the second corner and repeat the process around the cloth.

FINISHING

1 Press the embroidery lightly on the wrong side. Pin and tack a double 2.5 cm (1 in) hem (page 136) round the cloth and mitre the corners (page 140). Make sure that the embroidered border is an equal distance from the hem edge along each side of the cloth. Hand sew the hem (page 136).

2 To complete the cloth, work a row of spaced running stitches (page 134) round the cloth 2 cm (¾ in) from the edge in two strands of light shaded pink (62).

RIGHT: Each coloured square represents one cross stitch worked over three vertical and three horizontal woven blocks of fabric. The black lines indicate details worked in back stitch over three blocks.

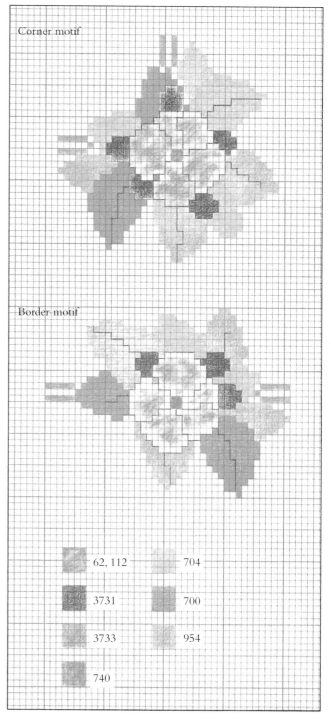

Corner motif

Border motif

	62, 112		704
	3731		700
	3733		954
	740		

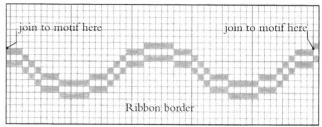

join to motif here   join to motif here

Ribbon border

TULIP BEDLINEN

Personalize plain, ready-made pillowcases and a duvet cover with embroidered tulip motifs in two sizes. Stitched in shades of pink, green and blue to contrast with pale green fabric, this design uses the waste canvas technique, which enables counted thread stitches to be worked neatly on ordinary fabric.

MATERIALS
- 2 ready-made pale green pillowcases and matching double duvet cover
- 68 cm (27 in) wide 10 count double thread waste canvas
- DMC stranded cotton: see the thread list below
- Tapestry needle size 24
- Tacking thread in a dark colour
- Sewing needle and pins
- Matching sewing thread
- Embroidery hoop

THREAD LIST

604	light pink	3760	mid blue
962	mid pink	320	soft green
3607	dark pink	701	mid green
3755	light blue	907	lime green

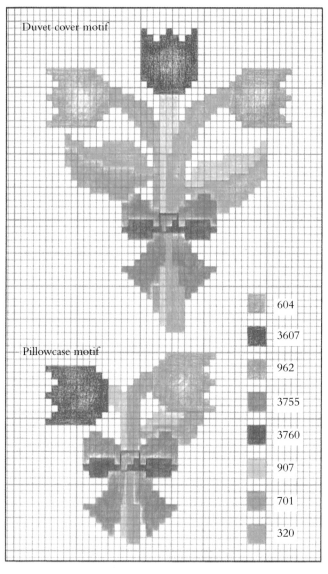

Duvet cover motif

Pillowcase motif

| 604 |
| 3607 |
| 962 |
| 3755 |
| 3760 |
| 907 |
| 701 |
| 320 |

PREPARING THE FABRIC

PILLOWCASE

The small tulip design on the pillowcase is positioned near the open end. The design covers an area 27 squares wide and 29 squares deep and each coloured square represents one cross stitch worked over one vertical and one horizontal double canvas thread. Count out and cut a rectangle of waste canvas about 10 double threads larger all round than the design and mark the centre with a pin. Tack the canvas to the pillowcase, positioning it so that the centre of the design is 14 cm (5½ in) from both the open end and the top of the pillowcase. Mark the centre of the chart with a soft pencil.

DUVET COVER

One large tulip design is used at each side of the duvet cover. To be able to work the embroidery comfortably, you first need to unpick the top seam and a short distance down each side seam. The design covers an area 39 squares wide and 46 squares deep and each coloured square represents one cross stitch worked over one vertical and one horizontal double canvas thread. Count out and cut two rectangles of waste canvas about 10 double threads larger all round than the design, and mark the centres with pins. Tack one piece of canvas to each end of the top of the cover, positioning them so that the centre of the design is 23 cm (9 in) from the top seam and 30 cm (12 in) from the side seams. Mark the centre of the chart with a soft pencil.

LEFT: Use the small tulip design to decorate a corner of each pillowcase and repeat the larger design at each side of the duvet cover. If you prefer to use a sheet and blankets, work one large motif at each side of the sheet, positioning them so that the embroidery will show when the top of the sheet is turned down over the blankets.

ABOVE: This design is worked by the waste canvas method, where a piece of canvas is tacked onto plain fabric to provide a grid for working cross stitch neatly and accurately. Each stitch is worked through both the canvas and the fabric, then the canvas threads are removed after all the embroidery has been completed.

WORKING THE EMBROIDERY

PILLOWCASE AND DUVET COVER

1 Mount the fabric in the embroidery hoop (page 132), and work the design in cross stitch (page 134) from the chart, using three strands of thread in the needle throughout. Start stitching at the centre of the design and work outwards, remembering that each square on the chart represents one cross stitch worked over one vertical and one horizontal double thread of canvas. Take care to count the stitches accurately.

2 Following the chart, outline the centre of each bow in back stitch (page 134) using two strands of dark blue (3760) and working each back stitch over one pair of canvas threads.

FINISHING THE BEDLINEN

1 Press the embroideries lightly on the wrong side over a well-padded surface. Use a warm iron and take care not to press too hard and crush the stitching.

2 Carefully follow the detailed illustrated instructions on the right for removing the waste canvas threads from the bed linen.

3 Turn the duvet inside out and re-stitch the top and side seams together with matching thread. Turn the duvet right side out and give all the embroidered items a final light press.

USING WASTE CANVAS

This useful technique enables you to work counted cross stitch neatly and accurately on fabric which does not provide a natural grid for the stitching, due to its uneven weave. Canvas is a stiffened evenweave material normally used for needlepoint, but here it is temporarily attached to the fabric to provide a grid for the embroidery. You can buy special waste canvas which has coloured threads woven in at intervals to make counting simpler, or you can use ordinary needlepoint canvas, providing the threads are not interlocked. This technique will allow you to work any of the designs in this book on fabric which is not evenly woven, including towelling and sweatshirt fabric.

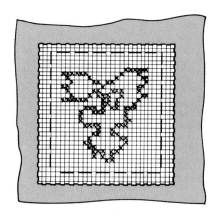

1 Choose canvas with the same count as the fabric suggested in the project instructions. Tack a piece of canvas on to the right side of the fabric, making sure it is large enough to allow the complete design to be worked. Work the cross stitch design over the canvas grid, taking the stitching through both canvas and fabric.

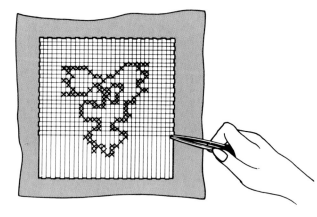

2 The fabric usually benefits from a light press before the waste canvas is removed, but take care not to crush the embroidery. Remove the tacking stitches and cut away the canvas close to the stitched design. Carefully pull out the canvas threads individually with a pair of tweezers, starting from one corner and gently pulling out all the threads which lie in one direction first. It may help to first moisten the canvas with water. Once all the threads running in one direction have been removed, pull out the remaining threads to reveal the finished design.

TRELLIS TIE-BACKS

Show off pretty cotton curtains by adding a pair of shaped, stiffened tie-backs embroidered with this stylish trellis and flowers pattern. Four template sizes are given to accommodate curtains made in different widths.

MATERIALS

- 130 cm (51 in) wide 18 count cream Aida evenweave fabric
- Cream cotton lining fabric
- DMC stranded cotton: see the thread list below
- Tapestry needle size 24
- Tacking thread in a dark colour
- Matching sewing thread
- Sewing needle and pins
- Adjustable rectangular embroidery frame
- Double-sided self adhesive pelmet stiffener
- Dressmaker's pattern paper
- 4 brass D-rings and 2 brass tie-back hooks

THREAD LIST

971	orange	702	green
444	yellow	704	light green

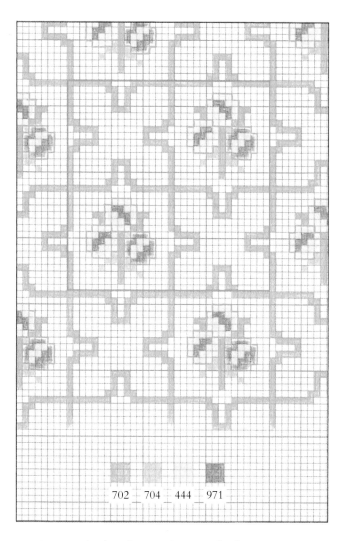

702 — 704 — 444 — 971

ABOVE: Each coloured square shown on the chart represents one stitch worked over two vertical and two horizontal woven blocks of fabric.

PREPARING THE FABRIC

Enlarge one of the templates on page 23 to the required size (see page 133), draw twice onto dressmaker's pattern paper and cut out. Lay both pattern pieces on the right side of the evenweave fabric and mark the areas to be embroidered by tacking round the outside of the patterns, 1 cm (½ in) away from the edge of the paper.

WORKING THE EMBROIDERY

1 Tack a vertical line through the centre of each tacked shape, taking care not to cross any vertical threads. Mark the central horizontal line in the same way. Mount the fabric in the embroidery frame (page 133).

2 Beginning at the centre of one tacked shape, work the repeating green trellis pattern in cross stitch (page 134) from the chart, using three strands of thread in the needle throughout. Work outwards, remembering that each square on the chart represents one cross stitch worked over two vertical and two horizontal woven blocks of fabric, until

the area inside the tacked lines is covered with trellis. Repeat the trellis pattern to cover the second shape.

3 Following the chart, work the flower motifs in alternate trellis squares in the same way as the trellis. To complete the embroidery, outline each flower in back stitch (see page 134), worked over two woven blocks of fabric, using two strands of thread in the needle.

FINISHING

1 To make up the tie-backs, first carefully remove the completed embroidery from the frame. Using a warm iron, press the embroidery lightly on the wrong side over a well-padded surface. Take care not to press too hard as this may crush the stitching and spoil the effect of the embroidery.

2 Cut out the embroidered pieces, allowing a margin of 1 cm (½ in) of unworked fabric all round the design.

3 Referring to the diagrams opposite, pin the paper pattern that was used previously onto double-sided, self-adhesive pelmet stiffener and cut around the shape twice. Also use the pattern to cut two shapes from the lining fabric, but this time add 1 cm (½ in) all round for turnings.

LEFT: Embroider the trellis and flowers pattern onto a cream or white background using colours which coordinate with your curtain fabric.

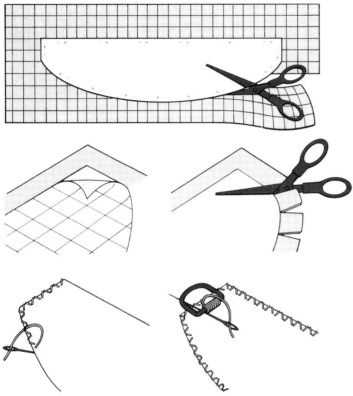

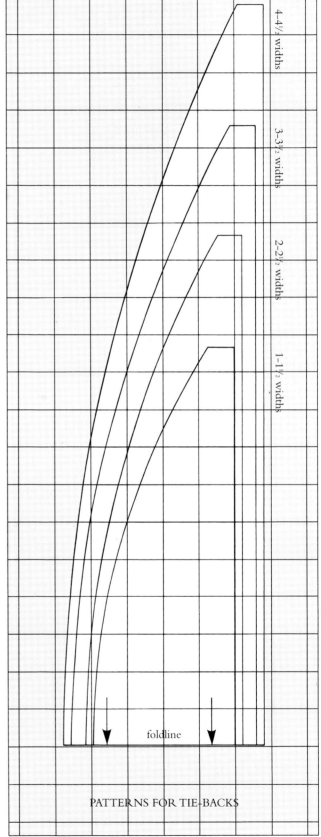

4 Peel the plain backing away from one side of the stiffener and position it on the wrong side of the embroidered fabric, leaving an even margin of fabric all the way round. Then turn the fabric over and smooth over with your fingers to eliminate any creases. Peel the graphed backing away from the stiffener.

5 Cut notches round the curved edge of the fabric, as shown, and fold the fabric over onto the self-adhesive surface of the stiffener, smoothing out any creases. Fold over the long straight edge and then the short edges.

6 Position the lining over the same side of the tie-back and stick in place. Turn under the raw edges of the lining all the way round, notching the curved edge, and slipstitch (see page 136) to the embroidered fabric. Repeat steps 4, 5 and 6 to make the second tie-back.

7 Sew a brass D-ring onto the lining at each end of the tie-backs. Fix a tie-back hook securely in position at each side of the window, then hang up the tie-backs.

4-4½ widths

3-3½ widths

2-2½ widths

1-1½ widths

foldline

PATTERNS FOR TIE-BACKS

BLUE AND WHITE CUSHION

To see freshly plumped-up cushions filling chairs and sofas around the home is, indeed, a simple luxury, and instantly suggests comfort and relaxation. Perhaps this is a throwback to the past when ornamental cushions were a symbol of wealth and status. Today, however, we tend to choose the type of cushion best suited to the decorative style of a room. Blue and white designs, such as the Chinese Willow Pattern and Delft tiles, have long been popular and were the inspiration for this cushion. The cross stitched sprigs of berries are offset with a deep border of bold blue and white checked fabric, which is also used for the back of the cushion. Two decorative bows secure the cushion closure at the centre back. The finished cushion measures 46 cm (18 in) square.

MATERIALS

- 41 cm (16 in) square 25 count white linen
- 41 cm (16 in) square white cotton for backing the linen
- Tacking thread
- Tapestry needle size 26
- Embroidery hoop (optional)
- DMC stranded cotton: see the thread list below
- 60 cm (24 in) by 137 cm (54 in) wide blue and white checked cotton
- Matching sewing threads
- 33 cm (13 in) square cushion pad

THREAD LIST

3747 pale blue	797 dark blue
793 dusty blue	

WORKING THE EMBROIDERY

1 Mark the centre of the linen fabric both ways with tacking stitches. Then mark the squares for the outer four motifs by counting 51 stitches (102 fabric threads) in each direction from the middle, and tack. Finally mark and tack the centre positioning lines in the four outer squares (see positioning diagram).

2 Work the embroidery in a hoop (see page 132) or in the hand, as preferred. Following the colour key and chart (on page 27), where each square represents one cross stitch worked over two fabric threads, and using two strands of thread in the needle throughout, begin the cross stitching in the middle with motif B. Complete motifs A and C following the positioning diagram given on page 26. Work all the cross stitching and finish by adding the backstitch details on top. Lightly press on the wrong side if needed.

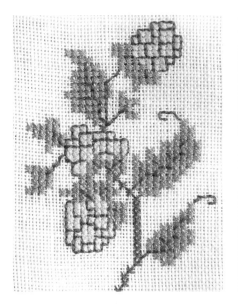

3 Trim the fabric evenly to measure 33 cm (13 in) square. This includes 12 mm (½ in) seam allowances, which are used throughout the cushion cover. Using three strands of blue (793), and 6 mm (¼ in) long running stitches, stitch the grid lines between the motifs (spaced 10 cm [4 in] apart) and around the edge (see the positioning diagram below).

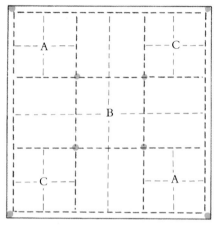

● Placement of tufts

ABOVE: Positioning diagram.

4 Using blue (793), wind the thread around a pencil several times. Cut off, thread the end into a needle, wind twice around the threads and knot it securely. Remove the threads from the pencil and attach them to the cushion front at the intersecting points as marked on the chart. Cut through the loops, trim and flatten to make the tufts. Repeat seven more times.

ABOVE: Tuft stitched on at marked intersection.

FINISHING

1 From the checked fabric cut out the following: for the border, four pieces 48 x 10 cm (19 x 4 in) and four pieces 33 x 10 cm (13 x 4 in); for the backing, two pieces 33 x 22 cm (13 x 8½ in); for the ties, four pieces 30 x 5 cm (12 x 2 in).

2 On one back section, make a 12 mm (½ in) hem on one long edge. On the second back section, turn under 12 mm (½ in) and then 3 cm (1¼ in), stitch and press. To make the back opening, lay the back sections flat with right sides uppermost and the hems adjacent to each other. Overlap the hems so that the deeper hem is below and the back measures 33 cm (13 in) square.

3 Make the ties by folding each piece of fabric lengthways in half and stitch around two sides taking a 6 mm (¼ in) seam. Turn right sides out, and press. Attach the ties in pairs to the back opening, stitching them directly opposite each other and placing them 8 cm (3 in) in from the outer edge. Tack the overlapped edges of the back pieces.

4 To attach the border, place two of the shorter pieces on opposite sides of the embroidery, right sides together and with raw edges matching. Pin and stitch. Press the seams towards the border. Attach two of the longer pieces in the same way and press. Repeat on the back section. Place the front and back together with right sides facing and stitch around the edge. Trim across the corners, turn the cover through the back opening and press the seam. Stitch around the inside edge of the border through both layers, sinking the stitching through the previous line of stitches.

ABOVE: Tied back of cushion.

3747

797

793

● tufts

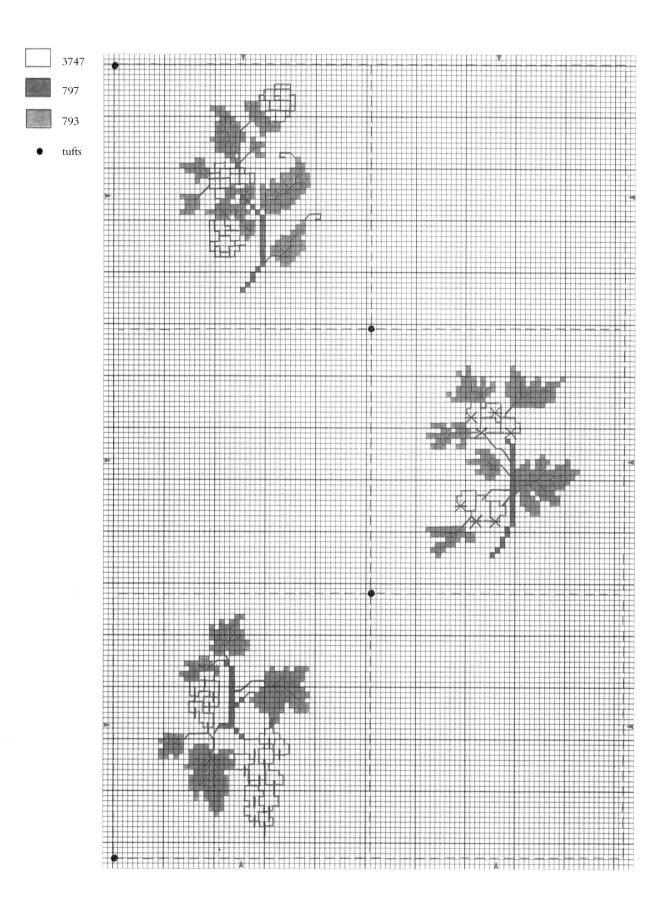

FLORAL
PATTERN LIBRARY

The following pages contain designs for alternative floral motifs, patterns and borders you could use in your cross stitch embroideries. You do not have to stick to the designs given in the projects, but instead can draw inspiration from these pages to create your own unique decorations. Why not try using the flower sprigs in place of the motifs in the blue and white cushion project, or embroider one of the floral bunches on your bedlinen?

FLOWER SPRIGS AND FRAMES

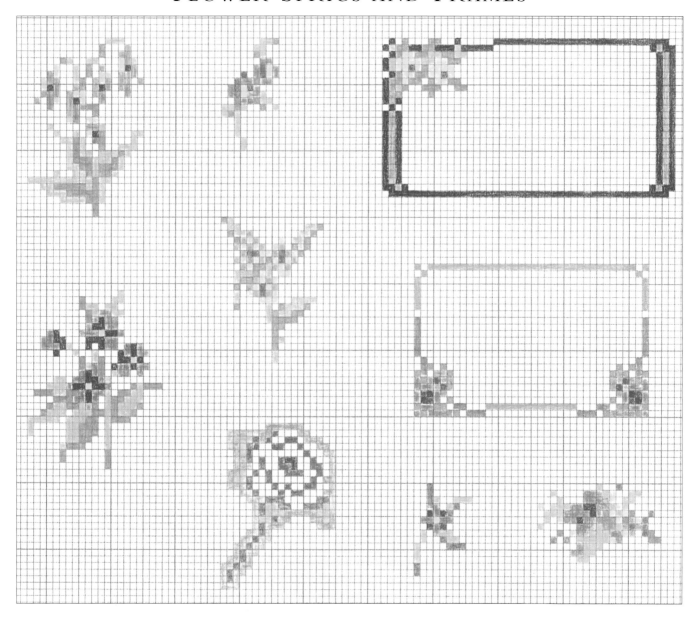

SPRIGS AND BUNCHES

FLOWERHEADS AND JUG OF FLOWERS

LARGE FLOWERS

ALL–OVER PATTERNS AND BORDERS

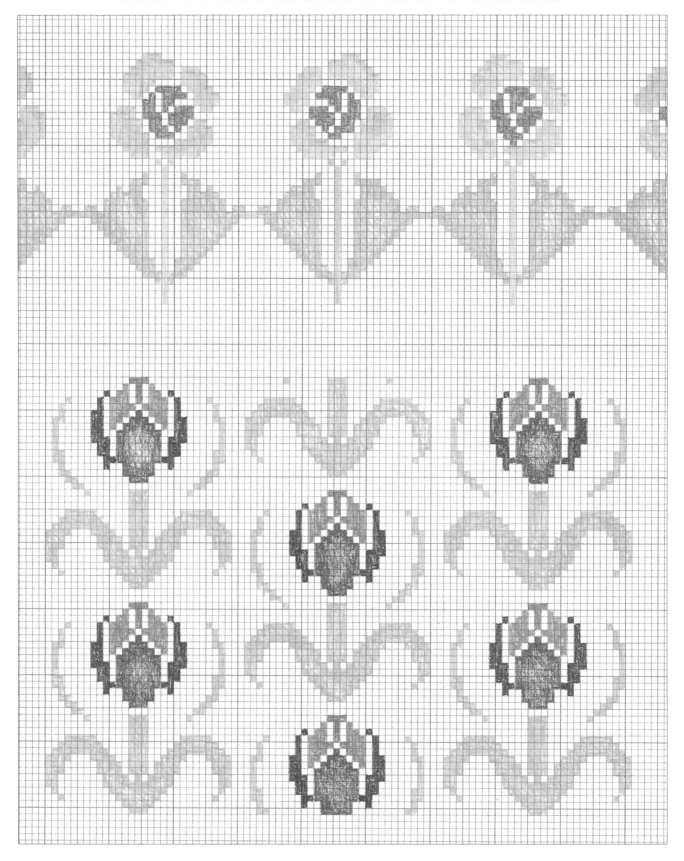

ALL–OVER PATTERNS AND BORDERS

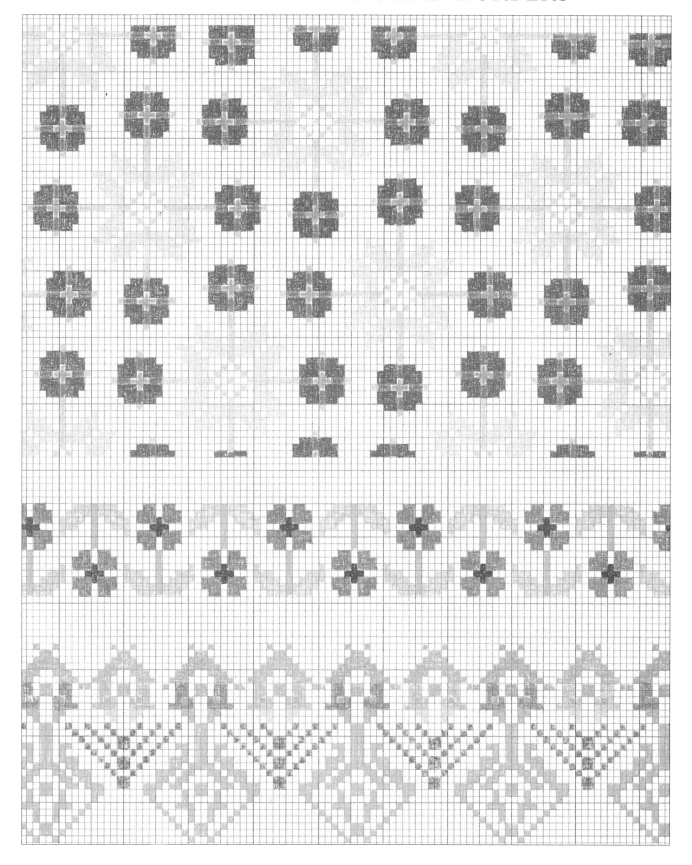

FOLK ART TABLE SETTING

*These striking red and blue folk art motifs
are quick and easy to stitch. Here, the two
motifs decorate a tablemat and napkin, but
experienced stitchers could use either of the
designs to make a border round a tablecloth.
Why not make a complete matching set?*

MATERIALS

- 130 cm (51 in) wide 18 count cream Aida
  even-weave fabric
- DMC stranded cotton: see the thread list below
- Tapestry needle size 24
- Tacking thread in a dark colour
- Sewing needle and pins
- Small embroidery hoop

THREAD LIST

498	deep red	712	pale cream
797	dark blue		

PREPARING THE FABRIC

TABLEMAT

1 This folk art pattern is adaptable to any size of place
setting. To decide on the best size for your
requirements, lay out a standard place setting of cutlery with
two sizes of plate. You may like to include space on the
tablemat for glasses and a side plate or place these items at
the edge of the mat. Measure the area used and add 2.5 cm
(1 in) all round for the hem allowance.

2 Tack two parallel guidelines to mark the position of
the embroidery. Here, the band of motifs is placed
about 2.5 cm (1 in) from the finished edge, and the band
itself is worked over 38 woven blocks of fabric. You can
extend the band right up to the finished edge on the two
long sides, or position it centrally as shown, whichever suits
your preference.

NAPKIN

1 Napkins are usually square, varying in size from small
tea napkins of 30 cm (12 in) to large dinner napkins of
60 cm (24 in). However, a good all-purpose size is 38 cm
(15 in) square. Lengths of 130 cm (51 in) width fabric can
be divided evenly for napkins of this size with sufficient left
for hem allowances after trimming away the selvedges. From
a 90 cm (36 in) length of fabric, you can cut six napkins.

2 Mark the position of the motif approximately 2.5 cm
(1 in) from the finished edges on two adjacent sides.

WORKING THE EMBROIDERY

1 Mount the fabric for the tablemat in the embroidery
hoop (page 132), and begin stitching at the centre of
the two tacked lines. Work in cross stitch (page 134) from

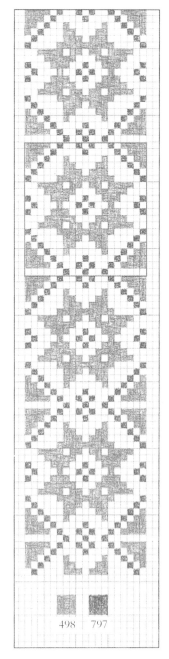

498   797

the chart, using three strands of thread in the needle throughout. Each square on the chart represents one cross stitch worked over two vertical and two horizontal woven blocks of fabric.

2 Work the napkin motif in exactly the same way as the tablemat motif.

FINISHING

1 Press the embroidery lightly on the wrong side. Cut away any surplus fabric round the tablemat, allowing a margin of 2.5 cm (1 in) for the hem allowance.

2 Pin and tack a narrow double hem (page 136) round the edge. Secure with back stitches (page 134) worked close to the turned-over edge. Work each stitch over two or three blocks of fabric using three strands of cream (712).

ABOVE: Strongly contrasting thread colours add interest to a plain soup plate. You can achieve a different effect by choosing a more subtle colour combination to harmonize with your own crockery, perhaps using a light and dark tone of the same colour.

Napkin

JAPANESE SCATTER CUSHIONS

Based on Sashiko quilting, a type of traditional stitching worked in Japan, the strong geometric patterns are easy to work providing you take care to count the stitches in each section accurately.

MATERIALS

- 110 cm (43 in) wide 14 count dark blue Aida evenweave fabric
- DMC stranded cotton: see the thread list below
- Tapestry needle size 24
- Tacking thread in a light colour
- Matching sewing thread and zip fasteners
- Ready-made cushion pads
- Sewing needle and pins
- Large embroidery hoop or adjustable rectangular embroidery frame

THREAD LIST

712 pale cream

PREPARING THE FABRIC

1 Decide on the finished size of each cushion cover, bearing in mind that you will need sufficient fabric to make both the front and back. On the front, add at least 10 cm (4 in) extra all round to allow you to mount the fabric in your embroidery hoop or frame. The plain back of each cover is made in two pieces joined by a central seam with a zip fastener inserted, so you will need to add 5 cm (2 in) for the seam allowances, plus 2.5 cm (1 in) all round for turnings.

2 Cut out the fabric for the front of each cushion and mark the finished size onto the fabric with lines of tacking, taking care that the lines of stitches run between two rows of woven blocks of fabric.

CUSHION A

The design for this cushion is worked in a central panel, leaving a wide margin of unworked fabric round the edge. First tack a vertical line through the centre of the fabric inside the tacked outline, taking care not to cross any vertical threads. Mark the central horizontal line in the same way. Mount the fabric in the embroidery hoop or frame (pages 132-133).

CUSHION B

The embroidery is worked in a broad band across the cushion, so first mark out this band by tacking two lines 78 fabric blocks apart. Then find the centre of this block by tacking a vertical line through the middle of the band, taking care not to cross any vertical threads. Then tack the central horizontal line in the same way. Mount the fabric in the embroidery hoop or frame.

CUSHION C

This cushion features an all-over design. First tack a vertical line through the centre of the fabric, taking care not to cross any vertical threads. Mark the central horizontal line in the same way. Mount the fabric in the the embroidery hoop or frame.

WORKING THE EMBROIDERY

CUSHION A

Begin working in cross stitch (page 134) at the centre of the fabric and work repeats of the design to form a square panel of four small squares across and down. Use four strands of thread and note that each pale square on the chart represents one stitch worked over two vertical and two horizontal woven blocks of fabric. Make sure you count the stitches accurately.

CUSHION B

1 Begin working in cross stitch (page 134) at the centre of the marked band and work repeats of the design until the band is filled. Use four strands of thread and note that each pale square on the chart represents one stitch worked over two vertical and two horizontal woven blocks of fabric.

2 Work approximately 1.5 cm (½ in) extra at each end of the band to avoid an unsightly gap in the embroidery when the cover is stitched together.

LEFT: Sashiko designs also lend themselves to many other colour combinations including black with pale grey, brown with gold and deep pink with apple green.

CUSHION C

1 Begin working in cross stitch (page 134) at the centre, repeating the design until the tacked area is filled. Use four strands of thread and note that each square on the chart represents one stitch worked over two vertical and two horizontal woven blocks of fabric.

2 Work approximately 1.5 cm (½ in) extra all round the cushion to avoid unsightly gaps.

FINISHING

The simplest way to make a plain cushion cover is to stitch the front and back pieces together round the edge, leaving an opening along one side. Slipstitch (see page 136) the opening closed after the filling has been added. On a larger cushion, it looks neater to close the opening with a zip fastener. When the cushion front has been embroidered right to the edge, insert the zip fastener in a seam across the cushion back for a really neat finish.

1 Press the embroidery lightly on the wrong side. Cut out to the required size, allowing 2.5 cm (1 in) all round for the seam allowance.

2 Pin the two back pieces together and position the seam either centrally or at one side of the fabric, stitching about 5 cm (2 in) at each end. Press the seams flat.

3 Pin, tack and machine stitch the zip fastener along the edge of the opening.

4 Open the zip fastener, place embroidered front and back together with right sides facing and stitch round all four sides of the cushion. Clip the corners to reduce bulk, then turn to the right side and press.

5 Insert the ready-made cushion pad and close the zip fastener.

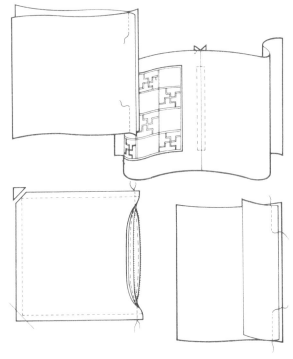

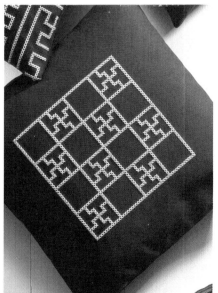

Cushion A

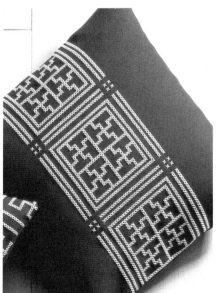

Cushion B

Cushion C

RIGHT: Cushion A: Although this design is intended to be worked in a central panel, it would be equally effective embroidered all over the front of the cushion cover in the same way as cushion C.

LEFT: Cushion B: This design would also look attractive stitched in bright colours of thread on white fabric. Try working the centre pattern in scarlet or emerald green, the outside stripes in royal blue and the single stitches in yellow.

RIGHT: Cushion C: Change the look of this design and work it in reverse by choosing a pastel shade for the background fabric and embroidering the lines with dark thread.

FOLK ART
PATTERN LIBRARY

The following pages contain patterns for alternative folk art borders and motifs and some traditional Japanese Sashiko designs. These can be adapted to fit any of the projects on the previous pages and are intended to give you further inspiration for your own embroidery creations.

FOLK ART BORDERS

FOLK ART BORDERS

FOLK ART MOTIFS

JAPANESE SASHIKO DESIGNS

CROSS STITCH FOR GIVING

*I COUNT MYSELF IN NOTHING
ELSE SO HAPPY
AS IN A SOUL REMEMBERING MY
GOOD FRIENDS.*

Richard II
WILLIAM SHAKESPEARE

BABY'S FIRST JACKET

Baby clothes are always a welcome gift and this little linen and voile-lined jacket, with its delicately embroidered flowers and lace trim, is pretty enough for a christening. The pattern is based on a traditional Magyar style from Hungary where the sleeves and jacket are cut in one piece. It is also one of the easiest patterns to adjust for larger or smaller sizes. The jacket fits a 60 cm (24 in) chest and measures 25 cm (10 in) long.

MATERIALS

- Two 72 x 36 cm (28 x 14 in) pieces 36 count white evenweave linen
- Tacking thread
- Tapestry needle size 26
- Embroidery hoop
- DMC stranded cotton: see the thread list below
- Dressmaker's graph paper
- Two 72 x 36 cm (28 x 14 in) pieces white voile
- White sewing thread
- 110 cm (43 in) of pre-gathered cotton lace, 2 cm (¾ in) wide
- 60 cm (24 in) of contrast ribbon, 1 cm (⅜ in) wide
- Two 1 cm (⅜ in) buttons

THREAD LIST

745	pale yellow	794	light dusty blue
725	mid yellow	793	dusty blue
722	peach	472	light moss green
554	pale mauve	3347	dusty green

WORKING THE EMBROIDERY

1 Cut one piece of linen widthways in half to give two jacket front pieces each measuring 36 cm (14 in) square. Referring to the chart, tack the positioning lines for the embroidery on one of the pieces, placing the vertical line 8 cm (3 in) from the side edge and the horizontal line 8 cm (3 in) up from the bottom edge. Repeat in reverse for the second piece. Stretch the fabric in a hoop (page 132).

2 Following the colour key and the chart, where each square is equal to one stitch worked over three threads of fabric, begin the embroidery, working outwards from the centre using two strands of thread in the needle. Complete the cross stitching and then add the backstitch details. Repeat on the second front. Lightly steam-press on the wrong side but keep the tacking stitches in place.

FINISHING

1 Enlarge the pattern pieces on page 48 onto dressmaker's graph paper (see page 133). Seam allowances of 12 mm (½ in) are included. Transfer all construction marks and draw in the positioning lines for the embroidery, before cutting out. Lay the embroidered fronts right side up, pin the pattern on top with the positioning lines matching, then cut out. Remember to cut out the second front in reverse so that the embroidery is at the centre front of the jacket. From the second piece of linen, folded widthways in half, cut out the jacket back placing the centre back to the fold. Cut out the lining from the voile in the same way.

2 With the right sides of the jacket fronts and jacket back together, pin and machine-stitch across the shoulder and sleeve seams. Press the seams open. Join the side and underarm seams in the same way. Repeat for the lining.

3 Place the jacket and lining right sides together, pin and machine-stitch around the neck, down the front pieces and around the bottom edge in a continuous movement. Trim the seam to 6 mm (¼ in), clip into the curves and across the corners before turning to the right side through one open sleeve. Finger-press the seams flat.

4 Make 12 mm (½ in) turnings on the sleeve edges and slipstitch to secure, easing the lining inside the outer sleeve edge. Using matching sewing thread, topstitch around the edges of the jacket with small running stitches.

5 Trim the neck and sleeve edges with lace. Hem-stitch it in place and overlap the raw edges to neaten.

6 Cut the ribbon into two halves and attach to the front edges of the neck, sliding it under the loose edge of the lace trim and catching it with a stitch. Sew the buttons on top, stitching through all layers. Using four strands of thread, work yellow and blue French knots (page 135) around the neck and sleeves, placing them about 12 mm (½ in) apart.

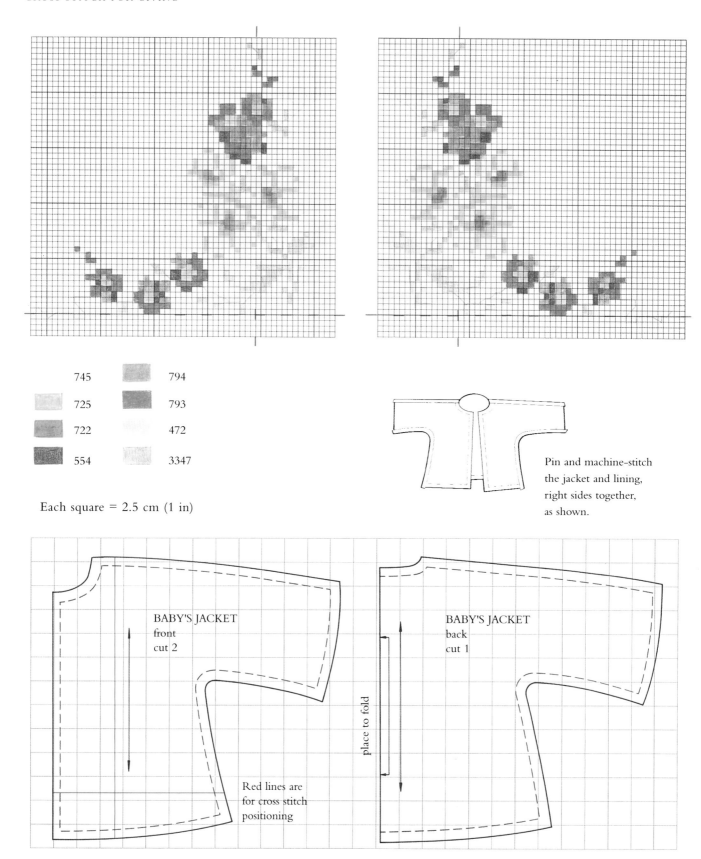

745

725

722

554

794

793

472

3347

Each square = 2.5 cm (1 in)

Pin and machine-stitch
the jacket and lining,
right sides together,
as shown.

BABY'S JACKET
front
cut 2

Red lines are
for cross stitch
positioning

BABY'S JACKET
back
cut 1

place to fold

BABY'S CRIB COVER

What better way to welcome a new baby than with beautiful gifts you have made yourself?
For this little crib or pram cover, which is based on a patchwork quilt construction, there
are decorative hearts in the squares with a different motif in each one to represent
good luck, joy, peace and tranquillity, as well as the baby's first names.
The finished cover measures 69 x 49 cm (27 x 19 ½ in) including the frill.

MATERIALS
- Metric graph paper
- Six 20 cm (8 in) squares 16 count white Aida
- Tacking thread
- Tapestry needle size 24
- Small embroidery hoop (optional)
- DMC stranded cotton: see the thread list below
- 1 m (40 in) by 152 cm (60 in) wide white broderie anglaise
- 2.7 m (3 yds) by 5 cm (2 in) wide white, pre-gathered broderie anglaise trim
- 66 x 47 cm (26 x 18½ in) medium-weight synthetic wadding
- White sewing thread
- 12 pearl buttons, 6 mm (¼ in) across (optional)

THREAD LIST
445	pale lemon yellow	472	light moss green
307	lemon yellow	907	lime green
742	light orange	913	viridian green
351	pale red	3042	pale aubergine
761	pale pink	3752	grey blue

WORKING THE EMBROIDERY

1 Following the alphabets on pages 52–53, draw your chosen name on metric graph paper or, alternatively, repeat two of the motifs given.

2 On each of the white Hardanger squares, which include a 2.5 cm (1 in) allowance all round, mark the centre both ways with tacking stitches and place in a small hoop, if preferred (see page 132).

3 Following the appropriate colour key and chart, where each square equals one cross stitch, complete the embroidery on all six squares, using two strands of thread in

the needle. Note that the butterfly wings are outlined in pale red (351); the veins of the clover leaves, the dove's wing and the rabbit's tail in pale aubergine (3042); the dove's body in light orange (742); the dove's tail and the rabbit's body in grey blue (3752).

4 Using the tacking stitches to measure accurately, trim the edges of the squares, leaving a 12 mm (½ in) seam allowance. Remove tacking. Steam-press on the wrong side.

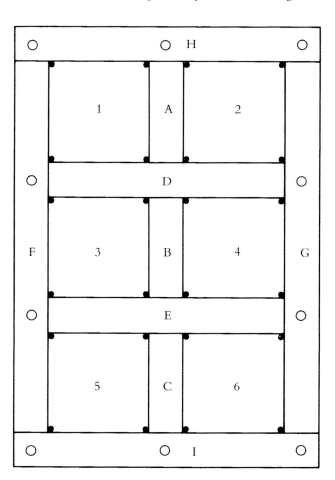

Positioning guide

FINISHING

1 From the broderie anglaise fabric, cut out the following pattern pieces: Crib cover back, 64 x 44.5 cm (25 x 17½ in); Crib cover front, cut two side pieces 56 x 6.5 cm (22 x 2½ in) [F and G on the positioning guide on page 49]; cut two pieces (top and bottom) 44.5 x 6.5 cm (17 ½ x 2½ in) [marked H and I]; cut two across pieces 37 x 6.5 cm (14½ x 2½ in) [marked D and E]; cut three short upright pieces 18 x 6.5 cm (7 x 2½ in) [marked A, B and C]. Seam allowances of 12 mm (½ in) are included.

2 Following the main picture and the positioning guide (page 49), lay out the embroidered squares in sequence and then the strips of broderie anglaise. Tack and machine stitch the three shorter rows across, beginning by joining together pieces 1, A, and 2. Stitch with the evenweave on top so that you can keep a straight line along the grain. Press the seams open. Join rows D and E in the same way. Then add F and G, followed by H and I to finish piecing the top.

3 Lay the backing fabric wrong side up, place the wadding on top and tack across both ways. Join the raw ends of the broderie anglaise trim using a small French seam (page 138). Lay the top section right side up, place the trim with the finished edge matching the raw edge of the fabric and tack to secure, easing extra fullness around the corners. Machine-stitch across one short edge.

4 Place the backing and top section with the right sides together, then tack and machine stitch around the edge of the cover, leaving a 23 cm (9 in) opening in one short side for turning through. Remove the tacking stitches, trim across the corners, and turn through to the right side. Lightly steam-press, if necessary. Turn under the seam allowance of the opening and slip-stitch to close.

5 Secure the three layers by tying quilting knots (see page 135) as marked on the positioning guide. With doubled thread in the needle, stitch through the layers, finishing with the knots on the wrong side. Attach the buttons, as shown.

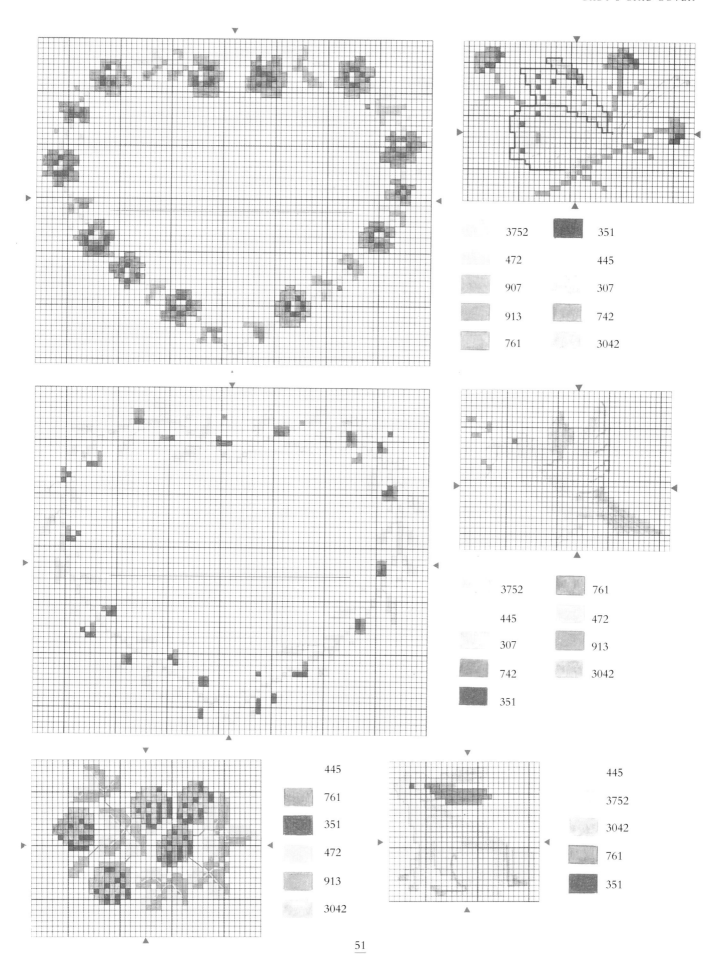

3752   351
472   445
907   307
913   742
761   3042

3752   761
445   472
307   913
742   3042
351

445
761
351
472
913
3042

445
3752
3042
761
351

ALPHABET FOR BABY'S CRIB COVER

BABY'S FIRST SLIPPERS

These delicate little slippers are made from fine white evenweave fabric, embroidered with the baby's initials on top and a cluster of rosebuds on the soles, as it is the feet, more often than not, that a baby in arms shows off rather splendidly. The slippers are one size, measuring 10 cm (4 in) along the length of the sole.

MATERIALS

- 30 cm (12 in) square 32 count fine white evenweave linen
- Tacking thread in a dark colour
- Embroidery hoop (optional)
- DMC stranded cotton: see the thread list below
- Tapestry needle size 26
- Tracing paper and pencil
- 46 cm (18 in) square white spotted voile for the lining
- 1 m (40 in) of white satin ribbon, 6 mm (¼ in) wide, for the ties
- Matching sewing thread
- Two pearl buttons, 6 mm (¼ in) across

THREAD LIST

927	pale grey green	326	deep pink
819	very pale pink	471	moss green
761	pale pink	3051	deep green
899	medium pink		

WORKING THE EMBROIDERY

1 You will find it easier to work the embroidery before cutting out the fabric. Select your chosen initials from the alphabet on pages 58–59. Following the positioning diagram on the right, fold the evenweave linen vertically in half. Using tacking stitches, mark the vertical central line and the horizontal positioning lines shown in blue on the diagram, then the centre lines on the slipper shapes marked in red on the diagram.

2 With your fabric stretched in a hoop, if preferred (see page 132), and two strands of thread in the needle, begin the embroidery, working one cross stitch over two threads of fabric. Follow the chart, where each square represents one stitch (i.e. two threads), making sure you match the centre of the chart with the red centre of your tacking stitches, then work outwards from the middle to complete the embroidery. Do not remove the tacking stitches: these are needed when you cut out the slippers.

FINISHING

1 Make paper templates for the sole and the slipper top by tracing around the patterns on page 57. Seam allowances of 8 mm (⁵/₁₆ in) are included. Mark the centre lines as indicated and cut out the templates. Pin each pattern piece over the embroidery, carefully matching the red centre lines, then cut out the fabric. Repeat for the second sole and slipper top. Remove all the tacking stitches.

2 To make the lining, fold the voile diagonally in half, crease the foldline and cut across. From one long edge, cut a 2.5 cm (1 in) wide bias strip for binding the slipper tops. From the remaining voile, cut two soles and two slipper tops on the straight grain.

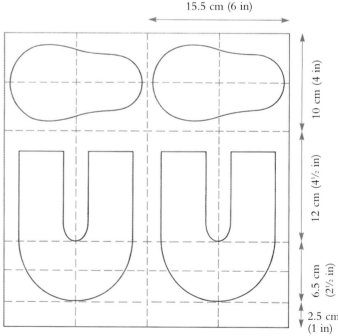

ABOVE: This positioning diagram shows how to work out the position of the embroidery on the fabric before the slipper shapes are cut out.

3 With the right sides together, machine stitch the centre back seam of each slipper top, then press the seam open. Matching the centres, pin each sole to the corresponding top and machine stitch around. Trim the seam to 6 mm (¼ in), snip into the curved seam allowance and turn to the right side. Finger-press the seam flat. Repeat for the lining but do not turn to the right side.

4 With the wrong sides together and the centres matching, place the lining inside the slipper, and tack around the top edge. Bind the top edge using the bias voile

strip. Beginning at the centre back seam, pin it to the right side, allow an extra 6 mm (¼ in) for the diagonal seam and cut to size. Join the bias strip (see page 139) and hand stitch the binding in place, using small running stitches. Fold the binding to the wrong side, turn under a 1 cm (⅜ in) hem and slipstitch to the wrong side.

5 Attach the ribbon ties. Cut the ribbon in half and stitch the centre of each tie to the centre back of the slipper, neatly overcasting the edges of the ribbon and binding on the wrong side. Sew a button in the centre of each tie.

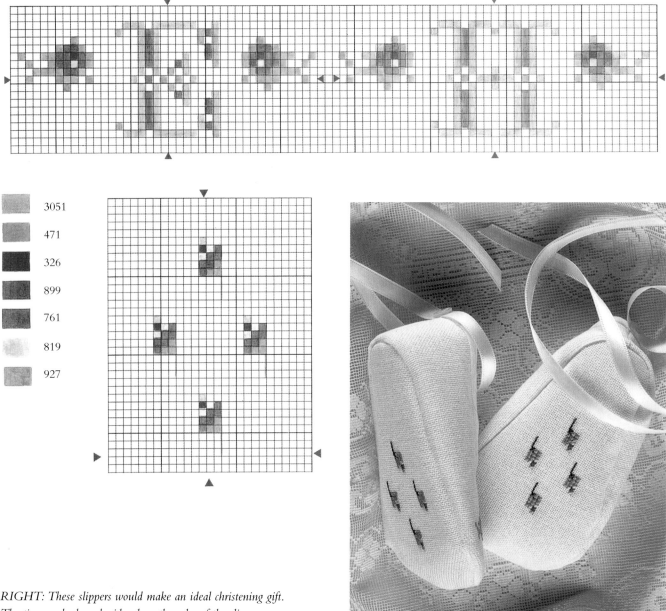

3051

471

326

899

761

819

927

RIGHT: These slippers would make an ideal christening gift. The tiny rosebuds embroidered on the soles of the slippers are a pretty and unexpected detail.

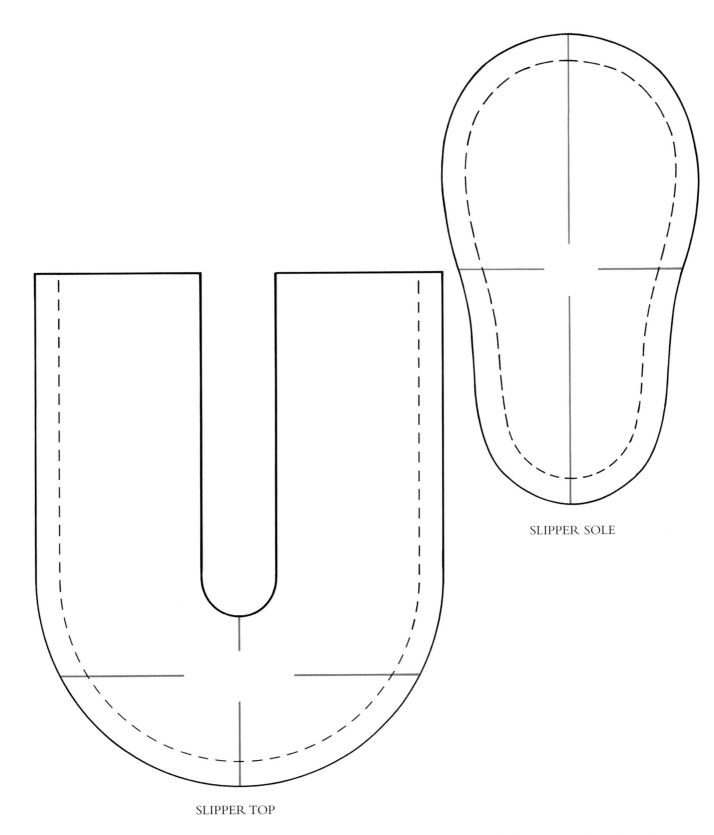

SLIPPER SOLE

SLIPPER TOP

ABOVE: Cut out one of each of these templates. They include an 8 mm ($^5/_{16}$ in) seam allowance. Mark the centre lines indicated in red.

ALPHABET FOR BABY'S FIRST SLIPPERS

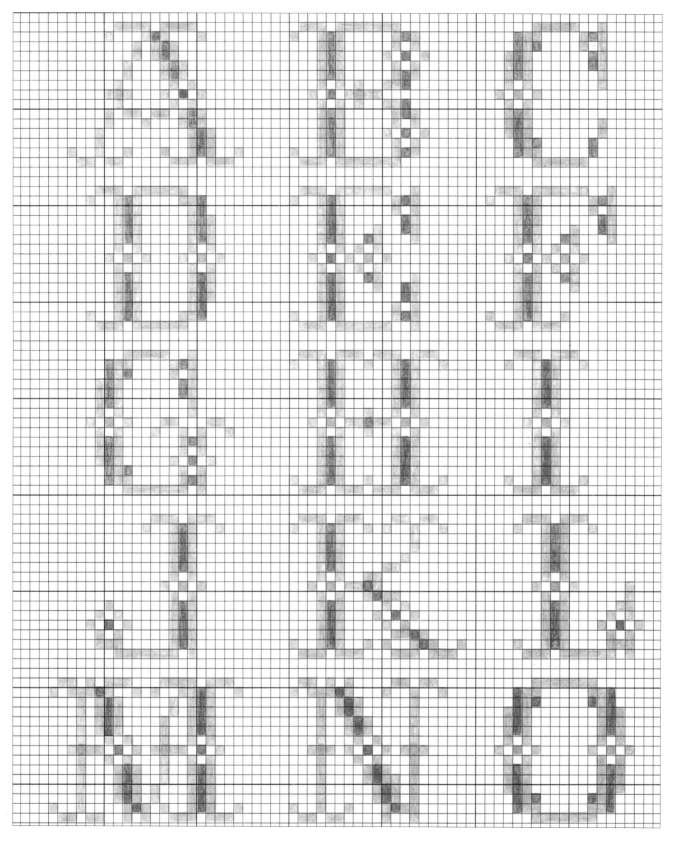

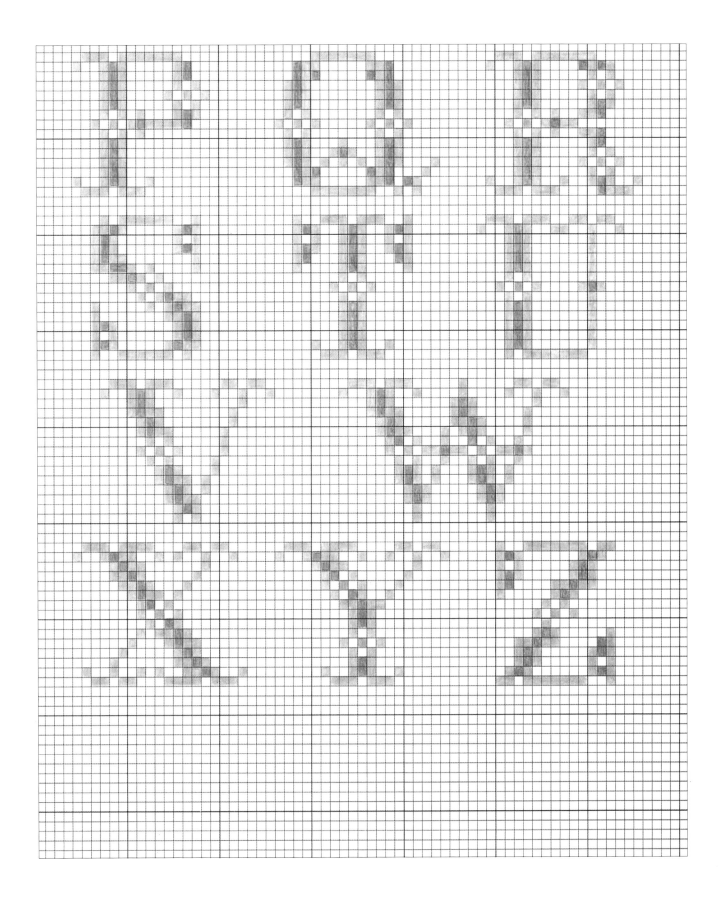

DOLL'S CRADLE QUILT AND PILLOW

This quilt and pillow cover design is based on patchwork, where pieces of different printed and woven fabrics are stitched together in geometric patterns. In old patchwork, the best parts of discarded garments would have been included and sometimes the colours were faded, which is an element included in this cross-stitched version. The small heart-print patches around the diamond are also a mixture of lighter and darker pinks. The finished quilt measures 23 cm (9 in) square and the pillow measures 11.5 x 7.5 cm (4¹/₂ x 3 in).

MATERIALS

- 25 count white evenweave fabric:
  two pieces 28 cm (11 in) square for the quilt and
  two pieces 18 x 13 cm (7 x 5 in) for the pillow
- Tacking thread
- Tapestry needle size 26
- Embroidery hoop (optional)
- DMC stranded cotton: see the thread list below
- 25 cm (10 in) square medium-weight
  synthetic wadding
- Matching sewing thread
- Crewel needle size 5

THREAD LIST

727	light medium yellow	3713	palest pink
742	light orange	760	pink
3820	deep golden yellow	472	light moss green
775	medium powder blue	703	medium green
3755	light blue	992	medium blue green
798	blue	731	olive green

WORKING THE EMBROIDERY

1 Both the quilt and the pillow are worked in the same way. On one of the two pieces of evenweave, mark the centre both ways with tacking stitches. Work the embroidery in a hoop (see page 132) or in the hand, as preferred.

2 Following the colour key and the appropriate chart (on page 62), where each square represents one cross stitch worked over two threads of fabric, begin the embroidery in the middle using two strands of thread in the needle throughout. Complete the embroidery and carefully steam press on the wrong side.

FINISHING

1 Trim the embroidery for the quilt, leaving 12 mm (¹/₂ in) seam allowances all around. Place it face down, centre the wadding on top and then lay the backing fabric (the second piece of evenweave) over the wadding, right side uppermost, carefully smoothing the layers in place. Pin and tack the layers together, stitching diagonally in both directions. Using a single strand of olive green (731) and following the stitch lines on the chart, quilt through all layers working outwards from the middle. Score the quilting lines using a ruler and tapestry needle. Using blue (798), quilt around the inner square (see chart).

2 Trim the wadding by 12 mm (¹/₂ in) all around. Turn under the seam allowances of the top and backing taking the top turning over the edge of the wadding. Pin and tack around the edge and, using matching thread, slipstitch to secure. Then, give your quilt a traditional finish by quilting close to the edge with matching thread.

ABOVE: Stitched and quilted cradle quilt.

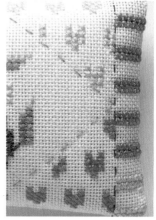

ABOVE: Stitched and quilted pillow.

3 To complete the pillow, trim the embroidery as for the quilt. Pin the wadding only behind the pillow top and, using a single strand of medium green (703), quilt around the diamond as shown on the chart. Using blue (798), quilt along the inside of the border.

4 Place the back and front together, right sides facing, pin and stitch around close to the embroidery, leaving one short side open. Trim the seam allowances, cut across the corners and turn through to the right side. Lightly stuff with teased-out wadding. Turn in the opening edges and slipstitch to close.

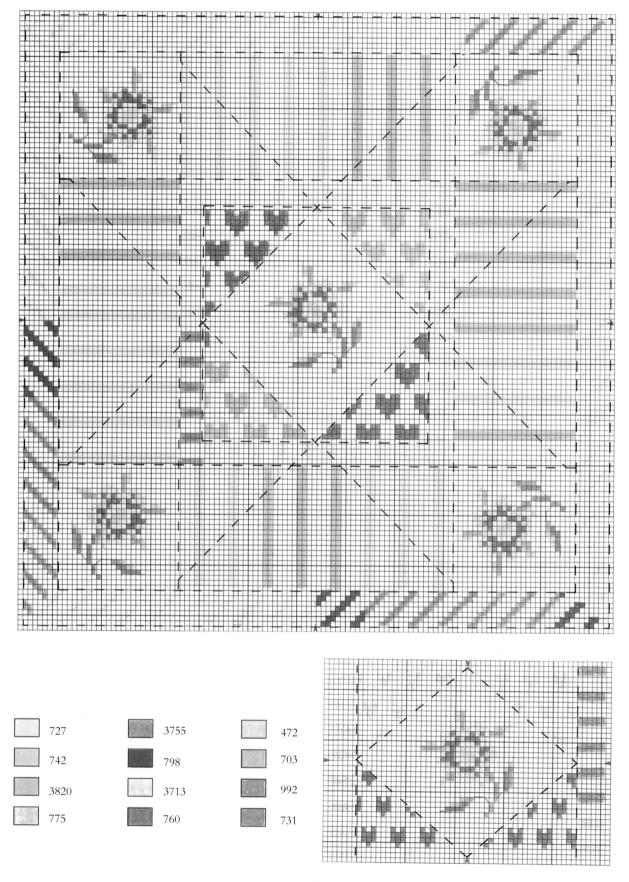

	727		3755		472
	742		798		703
	3820		3713		992
	775		760		731

NAIVE PAINTING

Inspired by the paintings of a group of amateur artists, who are primarily farmers, this is a simply-painted picture of a family pet rabbit translated into a cross stitch picture. The rabbit looks as though it has escaped from its hutch and is sittting in a well-tended, dark-coloured flowerbed. In its simply-stated outline, the rabbit possesses a certain power and beauty that is immediately attractive – something akin to primitive art. The finished unframed picture is 21.5 cm (8½ in) square.

MATERIALS

- 33 cm (13 in) square of 22 count red Hardanger
- Tacking thread
- Tapestry needle size 26
- Embroidery hoop (optional)
- DMC stranded cotton: see the thread list below
- 21.5 cm (8½ in) square of 3 mm (⅛ in) cardboard for mounting the embroidery
- 21.5 cm (8½ in) square of lightweight synthetic wadding
- Strong thread or masking tape for securing the mounted embroidery
- Picture frame of your choice

THREAD LIST

B5200	white	917	magenta
677	pale buff	472	light moss green
676	buff	471	moss green
445	pale lemon yellow	3012	light olive green
444	yellow	993	light blue green
3820	deep golden yellow	731	olive green
741	medium orange		

WORKING THE EMBROIDERY

1 Mark the centre of your fabric both ways with tacking stitches. Work the embroidery in a hoop (page 132) or in the hand, as preferred. Following the colour key and chart, where each square is equal to one cross stitch worked over two thread blocks, begin the embroidery in the centre, using two strands of thread in the needle.

2 Complete the cross stitching, working outwards from the centre. Finish the rabbit before moving on to the flowers and then the outer border. In white, add the background spots and the highlight on the rabbit's eye. Then backstitch the details on top using three strands of olive green (731) for the whiskers, and to outline the rabbit's ears and legs. Use two strands for the other backstitch details.

FINISHING

1 Lightly steam press the finished embroidery on the wrong side but leave the tacking stitches in place: they will be useful in centring the embroidery on the cardboard.

2 Mount your embroidery ready for framing following the instructions on page 141.

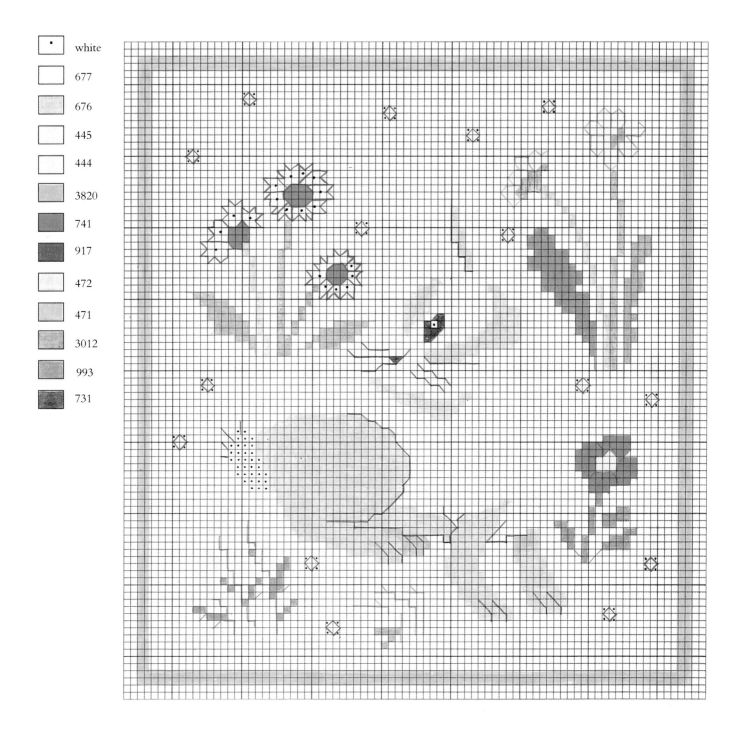

·	white
	677
	676
	445
	444
	3820
	741
	917
	472
	471
	3012
	993
	731

BUTTERFLY TOWELS

Decorate plain towels with rows of butterflies embroidered in soft pastel shades to
add a touch of summer to your bathroom.

MATERIALS

- 130 cm (51 in) wide 18 count cream Aida evenweave fabric
- Tapestry needle size 24
- Embroidery frame (optional)
- Cream towels with a woven band at each end
- DMC stranded cotton: see the thread list below

THREAD LIST

3733	dusty pink	517	light navy blue
210	mauve	798	blue
993	light blue green	813	sky blue
334	medium blue	966	soft powder green

PREPARING THE FABRIC

1 Measure the woven strip across your towels and add 1.5 cm (½ in) all round for turnings. Mark out the finished size of the bands on the fabric with rows of tacking, positioning the bands side by side and allowing sufficient fabric between them for turnings.

2 Find the centre of each band and mark with a pin. Mount the fabric in the embroidery frame (page 133).

WORKING THE EMBROIDERY

1 Referring to the chart below, work the butterflies in cross stitch (page 134), starting at the centre of the band and working outwards. Use three strands of thread in the needle.

2 To complete the design, work the details in back stitch (page 134) using three strands of thread.

FINISHING

1 Press the embroidered bands lightly on the wrong side with a warm iron. Take care not to crush the stitching. Cut out the pieces, allowing 1.5 cm (½ in) of unworked fabric outside the tacked lines.

2 Turn under the raw edges of each band, pin in place on the towel and secure with slipstitch (page 136).

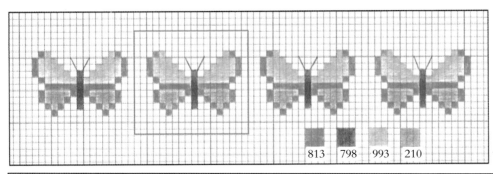

| 813 | 798 | 993 | 210 |

LEFT & BELOW:
Each coloured square represents one cross stitch worked over two vertical and two horizontal woven blocks. The coloured lines indicate rows of back stitch worked over two fabric blocks.

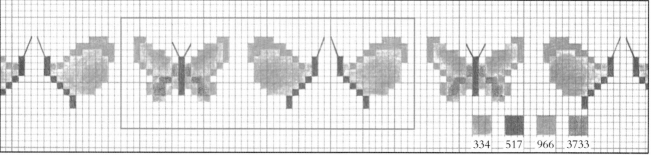

| 334 | 517 | 966 | 3733 |

ABOVE: Brighten up bath-time with these attractive matching towels. They make ideal guest-towels and children especially will love the pretty butterfly design.

NATURAL
PATTERN LIBRARY

The following pages contain designs for alternative borders and motifs with a natural theme. Any of the projects on the previous pages could be adapted to incorporate these ideas. Or you can simply use them for inspiration to create your own stitching patterns.

NATURAL BORDERS

NATURAL BORDERS

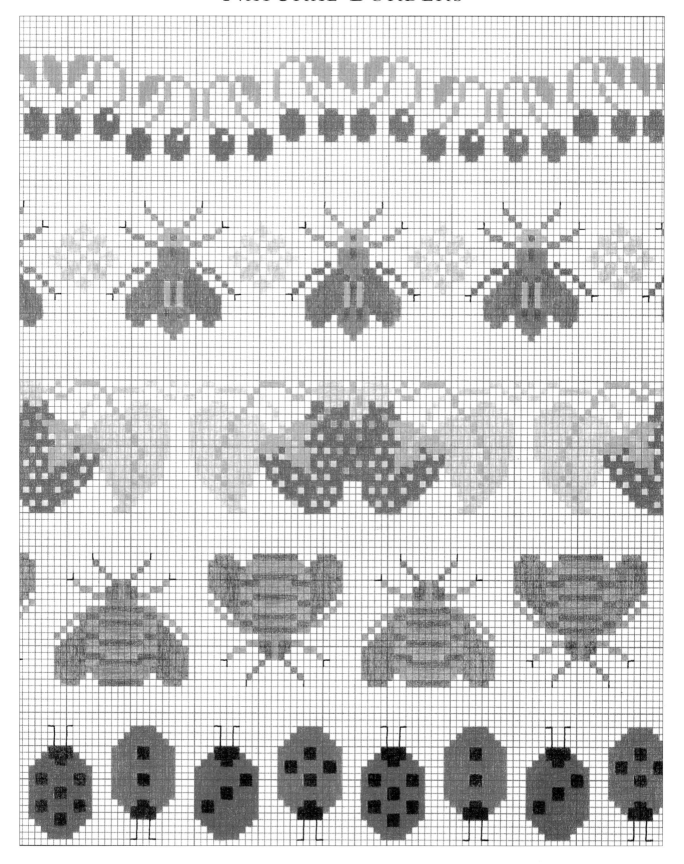

TREES ... AND A DOG

CATS ... AND A RABBIT

BIRDS AND BUTTERFLIES

SEA CREATURES AND BUTTERFLIES

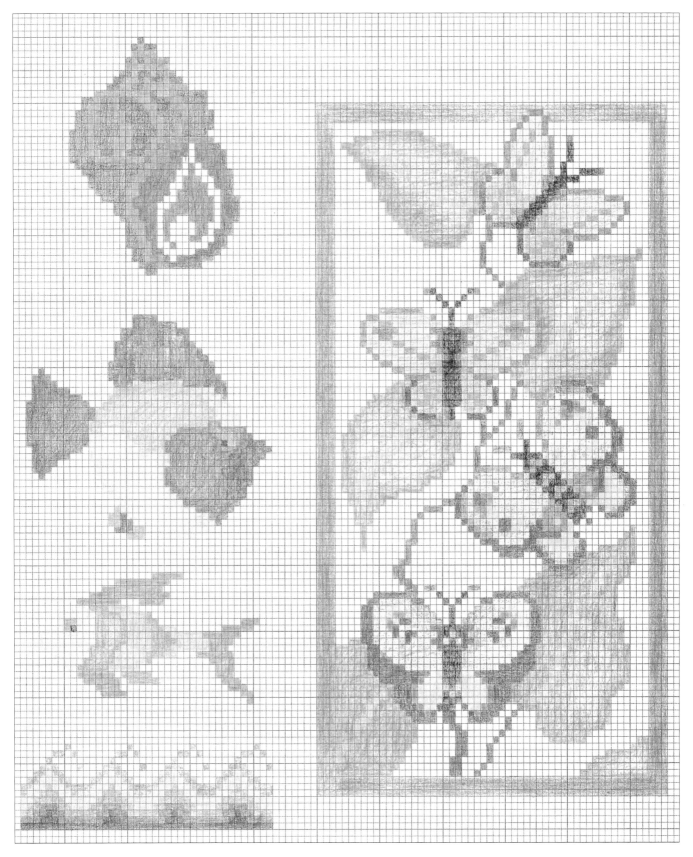

SLEEP PILLOW

A headrest filled with sweet-smelling herbs makes an ideal present for Mother's Day. One of the nicest fillings is a mixture of rose petals and a few drops of lavender oil. The filling is placed in a muslin bag before stitching it into the pillow cover, to prevent the crushed herbs from eventually coming through the cover in a powdery form. Openweave fabrics, such as Aida, are ideal for allowing the scent to permeate through. Interestingly, fragrant sleep-inducing stuffings go back to medieval times when mattresses were filled with straw and herbs. The finished pillow measures 24 x 22 cm (9½ x 8½ in).

MATERIALS

- 33 x 30 cm (13 x 12 in) of 14 count cream Aida fabric
- Tacking thread
- Tapestry needle size 24
- Embroidery hoop (optional)
- DMC stranded cotton: see the thread list below
- 27 x 24 cm (10½ x 9½ in) of cream cotton backing fabric
- Matching sewing threads
- Two 27 x 24 cm (10½ x 9½ in) pieces of white muslin
- Sufficient sweet-smelling herbs, rose petals and lavender oil or pot pourri to fill the pillow
- 27 x 24 cm (10½ x 9½ in) cushion pad (optional)
- 1.5 m (60 in) of two-colour contrast cord, 6 mm (¼ in) across
- Medium size sewing needle

THREAD LIST

772	palest dusty green	3042	pale aubergine
445	pale lemon yellow	224	pale damson pink
726	pale medium yellow	3354	light dusty pink
471	moss green	3688	medium rich pink
926	grey green	3687	rich pink

WORKING THE EMBROIDERY

1 Mark the centre of the Aida fabric both ways with tacking stitches. Work in a hoop or in the hand as preferred (see page 132).

2 Following the colour key and chart, where each square represents one stitch worked over one thread intersection, begin the embroidery. Work outwards from the centre, using two strands of thread in the needle. Ensure that you count the stitches accurately.

3 Complete the cross stitch and finish by working the backstitch details on top.

4 Retain the tacking stitches and lightly steam-press the finished embroidery on the wrong side.

FINISHING

1 Should the edges of the Aida fabric have frayed, use the tacking stitches as a guide to trim the edges evenly, keeping the embroidery centred, then trim further to the size of the backing fabric.

2 Place the front and back sections right sides together, tack and machine-stitch around, taking a 12 mm (½ in) seam and leaving a 15 cm (6 in) opening along one long edge. Trim across the corners and turn the cover through to the right side.

3 Make the muslin bag as for the outer cover, loosely fill with your chosen scented filling and then machine-stitch the opening together to close. Place the bag, or the cushion pad, inside the outer cover, turn under the raw edges of the opening and slipstitch to close, leaving a 2 cm (¾ in) gap.

RIGHT: You do not have to stick to the thread colours suggested here. It would be a nice idea to make up the cushion in colours to match your mother's bedroom decor, for instance.

4 Attach the cord around the edge. Slip one end of the cord into the gap in the seam and secure it with matching thread. Slipstitch the cord around the edge of the pillow, alternately catching the underside of the cord and sliding the needle under a few threads of the seam so that the finished stitching is completely hidden. Finish with the two ends neatly tucked into the seam; cross them smoothly and secure with a few well-hidden stitches. Secure the seam opening in the same way.

5 Make the tassels from the remaining cord. Cut four 8 cm (3 in) lengths. Fold one piece in half and, using matching sewing thread, attach it to a corner of the pillow, stitching it through the centre. Fold the cord and, with the thread, bind around both cords close to the stitching, then fasten off securely. Untwist the cord and fringe the threads to finish. Repeat on the other three corners of the pillow.

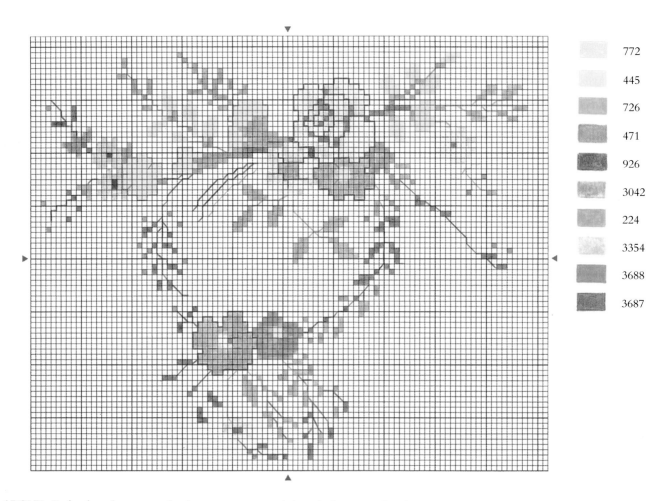

	772
	445
	726
	471
	926
	3042
	224
	3354
	3688
	3687

ABOVE: Each coloured square on the chart represents one stitch worked over one thread intersection.

CHINESE BLUEBIRDS OF HAPPINESS

Bluebirds denote happiness in Chinese mythology. In this picture, a pair of birds are set against a background decorated with the repeated symbol of longevity. This would make an ideal gift for a marriage celebration. The design is stitched mainly in shades of blue thread on white fabric, the traditional colours used for centuries in Chinese peasant cross stitch embroidery.

MATERIALS

- 110 cm (43 in) wide 11 count white Aida evenweave fabric
- DMC stranded cotton: see the thread list below
- Tapestry needle size 24
- Tacking thread in a dark colour
- Sewing needle
- Adjustable rectangular embroidery frame or rectangular wooden stretcher
- Sturdy cardboard
- Strong linen carpet thread or very fine string

THREAD LIST

333	bright purple	796	deep blue
340	dark lavender blue	798	blue
791	darkest blue	813	sky blue

PREPARING THE FABRIC

1 The embroidered area of the picture measures approximately 20 cm (8 in) square. To this you will need to add at least 10 cm (4 in) all round to allow for mounting the fabric in a frame in order to work the stitching, and to enable the finished embroidery to be laced round a piece of cardboard prior to framing. You may need to add a wider margin of fabric round the edge when working on a large embroidery frame or on a stretcher which cannot be adjusted.

2 Cut out the fabric and tack a vertical line through the centre of the fabric, taking care not to cross any vertical threads. Mark the central horizontal line in the same way and mark the centre of the chart with a soft pencil. Mount the fabric in the embroidery frame or stretcher (see page 133).

WORKING THE EMBROIDERY

1 Begin stitching at the centre of the design, noting that each coloured square on the chart represents one complete stitch worked over one woven block of fabric. Work the pair of bluebirds in cross stitch (page 134), using two strands of thread in the needle throughout.

2 When the birds have been completed, outline them and add the wing details in back stitch (page 134) using two strands of thread in the needle. Work each back stitch over one block of fabric.

3 Work the cloud outlines in back stitch using two strands of thread. Work carefully from the chart, stopping at intervals to check that the back stitch lines are in the correct position.

4 Finally, work the background pattern and border in cross stitch using three strands of thread in the needle.

FINISHING

1 When all the embroidery has been completed, press lightly on the wrong side over a well-padded surface. Use a warm iron and take care not to press down too hard and crush the stitching.

2 Decide on the size of the frame and window mount for the picture, and then lace the embroidery securely over a piece of sturdy card cut to the appropriate size (see page 141). Use strong linen carpet thread or very fine string for the lacing.

3 Place the mounted embroidery in your choice of frame behind the window mount and secure. See page 141 for ideas on framing embroidery.

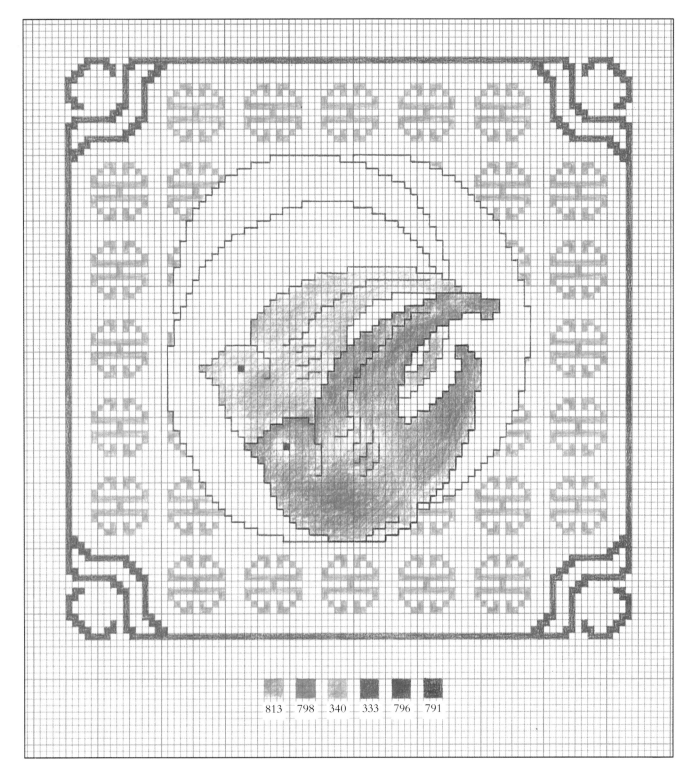

813	798	340	333	796	791

LEFT: This bluebird design could also be used to decorate a cushion or a photograph album cover. It would work well stitched in tapestry wool on canvas, but you would then have to stitch the background colour as well.

ABOVE: The backstitch outlines are indicated by blue lines on the chart. Work these after the birds have been completed.

CHESSBOARD

Chess continues to captivate players of all ages. This embroidered chessboard, framed under glass, would make a very acceptable gift on Father's Day. The finished unframed chessboard measures 40 cm (15³/₄ in) square.

MATERIALS

- 50 cm (20 in) of 20 count off-white linen
- Tacking thread
- Tapestry needle size 24
- Embroidery hoop or frame
- DMC stranded cotton: see the thread list below
- 40 cm (15¾ in) square of 3 mm (⅛ in) cardboard for mounting the embroidery
- 40 cm (15¾ in) square of lightweight synthetic wadding
- Masking tape or strong thread to secure the mounted embroidery
- Frame (with glass) of your choice

THREAD LIST

310   black (four skeins)   347   soft red (two skeins)

WORKING THE EMBROIDERY

1 Mark the centre of the linen both ways with tacking stitches. Stretch it in a hoop or frame (see pages 132–133) and begin the embroidery by backstitching the lines, working outwards from the centre.

2 All the embroidery, apart from the outer border, is worked in black using two strands of the thread in the needle throughout. Following the chart, where each square represents one stitch worked over two threads of fabric, backstitch the vertical lines first, then the horizontal lines to form a series of squares. Fill in alternate squares with the patterns, as shown on the chart. Work the two outer borders to complete one half of the board design and then turn the work around and repeat the design on the opposite side, to complete the embroidery.

FINISHING

1 Lightly steam-press on the wrong side, and retain the tacking stitches to help centre the embroidery when you mount it on cardboard.

2 Mount and frame the completed embroidery following the instructions on page 141.

   310

347

ABOVE: For the second half of the board, repeat the design in reverse from the vertical centre line.

BOOKMARK

Many young children are eager to make their own gifts, so this easy-to-make bookmark is ideal for younger cross stitchers. This is worked on a purchased evenweave band, where the edges are already finished, and the design uses just two colours so that children can easily substitute their own choice of colours to embroider on a bookmark as a special present for father. The tassel can be omitted, if preferred, and the point left plain and simple. The finished bookmark measures 24 x 5 cm (9 ½ x 2 in).

MATERIALS

- 23 cm (9 in) by 5 cm (2 in) wide 15 count cream prepared evenweave band
- Tacking thread
- Tapestry needle size 24
- DMC stranded cotton: see the thread list below
- Matching sewing thread

THREAD LIST

347 soft red   3765 dark turquoise blue

WORKING THE EMBROIDERY

1 Mark the centre of the fabric in both directions with tacking stitches.

2 Working in the hand, follow the colour key and chart, where each square is equal to one stitch, begin the cross stitching with the lettering, working outwards from the middle, using two strands of thread in the needle. Complete the embroidery and remove the tacking stitches.

FINISHING

1 Press on the wrong side. Make a small double turning on the top edge, folding the fabric to the wrong side; hem in place.

2 To point the lower edge, fold the bookmark lengthways in half, right sides together. With matching thread, back stitch across the short edge. Press the seam open and turn to the right side. Flatten out the bookmark to create the point, and slip stitch to secure.

3 Make the tassel by winding cream sewing thread around a piece of card about 3 cm (1⅛ in) wide. Thread the loose end into a needle, slip the tassel threads off the card and wind the loose thread several times around one end. Pass the needle up through the binding to emerge at the top of the tassel. Sew on to the point of the bookmark. Cut through the looped threads at the bottom of the tassel to complete.

LEFT: Adapt this design to suit your choice of lettering by using the alphabet pattern library on pages 123-127.

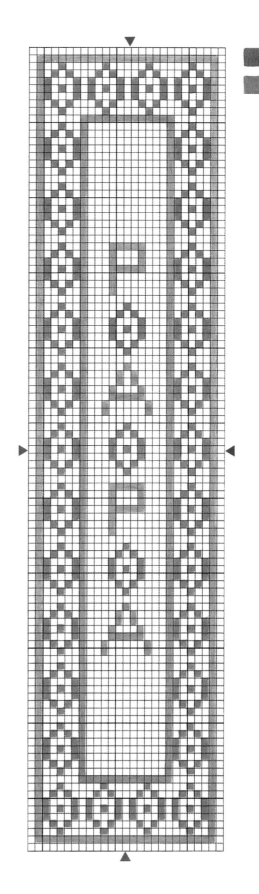

347

3765

FRIENDSHIP BRACELETS

The exchanging of fabric bracelets between friends is a charming custom. They are often made in the hand by finger-plaiting together different coloured yarns where the ends form a natural loop and tie. Once bracelets are exchanged, friendship is forever. For the friendship to endure, the bracelet should never be removed from the wrist or ankle, or wherever it may be worn. As friendship bracelets can so easily be made from the smallest scrap of fabric, and involve a minimum of cross stitching, even beginners to embroidery might be tempted to try their skill. The finished bracelets measure 19 x 2 cm (7 1/2 x 3/4 in), without the ties.

MATERIALS

- 25 x 6 cm (10 x 2½ in) 28 count red evenweave fabric
- 25 x 6 cm (10 x 2½ in) 28 count cream evenweave fabric
- Tacking thread
- Tapestry needle size 26
- Embroidery hoop (optional)
- DMC stranded embroidery cotton: see the thread lists below
- Small gold beads for the red bracelet (optional)
- Crewel needle size 6
- Matching sewing threads

THREAD LIST

RED FABRIC		CREAM FABRIC	
725	medium yellow	3821	medium golden yellow
501	dark grey green	3354	light dusty pink
		3805	bright pink
		503	medium grey green

WORKING THE EMBROIDERY

1 Both bracelets are embroidered in the same way. Mark the centre of the fabric both ways with tacking stitches. Work the embroidery in a hoop (see page 132) or in the hand, as preferred. Small amounts of fabric such as these are easier to work in the hand. Following the appropriate colour key and chart (see page 87), where each square is equal to one stitch worked over two fabric threads, begin the cross stitching working outwards from the centre. Use two strands of thread in the needle throughout.

2 On the red bracelet, begin with the larger diamond in the middle using dark grey green (501). Complete the green cross stitching and add the medium yellow (725) diamonds in between. Sew a gold bead to the centre of each large green diamond. Remove the tacking threads and lightly steam-press on the wrong side.

3 On the cream bracelet, begin with the zigzag pattern, and then outline the bracelet using medium grey green (503). Fill in the triangular patterns to complete the embroidery.

FINISHING

1 Trim the long edges of the fabric leaving 2 cm (3/4 in) at each side of the embroidery (also 2 cm (3/4 in) wide). Trim the two short sides to within 6 mm (1/4 in) of the embroidery.

2 To make the pointed ends, follow the diagrams on page 86 and fold over the short end by 6 mm (1/4 in), then fold in each corner to the centre and press flat. Repeat at the other end.

3 Make a loop and single tie by plaiting together three 15 cm (6 in) lengths of embroidery thread in mixed colours, using six strands each. Cut off 6.5 cm (2½ in), fold in half to make the loop and bind the cut ends securely. Bind the cut end of the remaining plait for the tie.

4 Insert the bound end of the loop under the folds at one pointed end and the tie under the other. Pin and slip stitch the folds together (page 136), oversewing the plaits very securely at each point.

5 Fold one long edge over, taking a 2 cm (¾ in) turning. Make a 1 cm (⅜ in) turning on the opposite side and fold it over the first turning. Pin, tack and decoratively cross stitch to hold along the centre seam, stitching through the folded layers only. Using matching thread, top stitch the edges of the bracelet with running stitches. Remove the tacking and repeat for the second bracelet.

Diagram 1

2 cm (¾ in)

2 cm (¾ in)

1 cm (⅜ in)

1 cm (⅜ in)

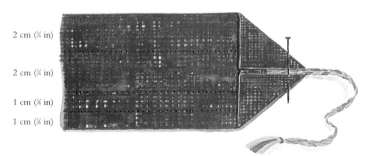

Diagram 2

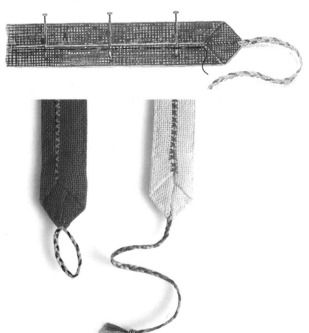

ADAPTING THE BASIC FRIENDSHIP BRACELETS

The combination of ground fabric colours and stitched motifs is endlessly variable. Take inspiration from the designs given or create your own patterns. Experiment by changing the colour of the ground fabric, for example, to give totally different effects. The longer designs given here are intended for a friendship choker and anklet but they can easily be made shorter for a bracelet, if preferred. The finished choker measures 31 x 2 cm (12 x ¾ in); the anklet measures 20 x 2 cm (8 x ¾ in).

MATERIALS
- For the choker: 38 x 6 cm (15 x 2½ in) of 27 count black evenweave fabric
- For the anklet: 28 x 6 cm (11 x 2½ in) of 27 count white evenweave fabric
- Tacking thread
- Tapestry needle size 26
- Embroidery hoop (optional)
- DMC stranded cotton: see the thread lists below

THREAD LIST

CHOKER		ANKLET	
725	medium yellow	958	mint green
891	light red	917	magenta
3811	light turquoise	792	deep dusty blue

MAKING THE CHOKER AND ANKLET

1 Referring to the colour key and the charts given on the right and following the instructions for the basic bracelet, complete the embroidery. Ensure that you count the stitches accurately or you could spoil the overall effect of the design.

2 Make two plaited ties using three 20 cm (8 in) lengths of embroidery thread. Insert the ends into the folded ends of the choker or anklet and secure as for the bracelet. Tie in a bow to hold in place.

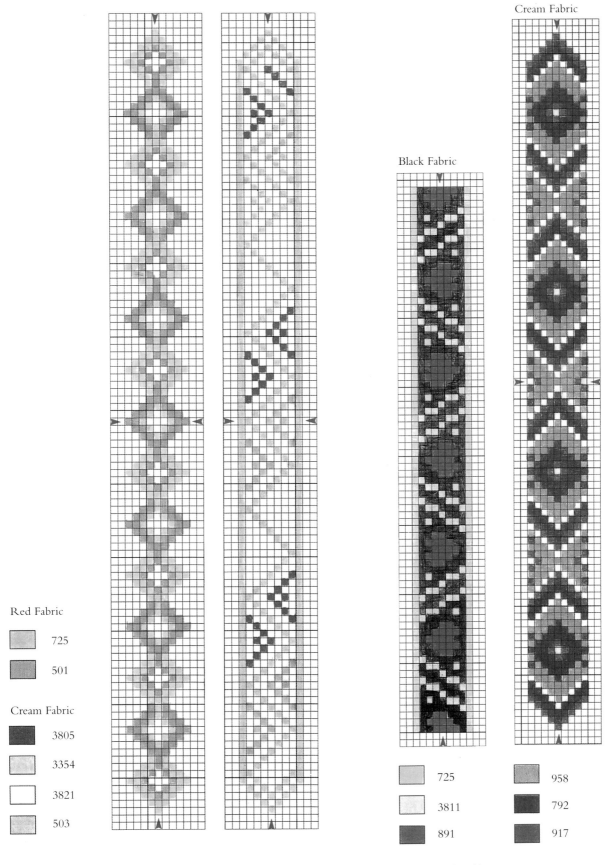

Cream Fabric

Black Fabric

Red Fabric

	725
	501

Cream Fabric

	3805
	3354
	3821
	503

	725		958
	3811		792
	891		917

ABOVE: Basic Friendship Bracelets.

ABOVE: Choker and Anklet.

GEOMETRIC PATTERN LIBRARY

The following pages contain geometric motifs, border designs and repeat patterns for you to draw inspiration from and work into your own embroidery designs.

BORDERS AND CORNERS

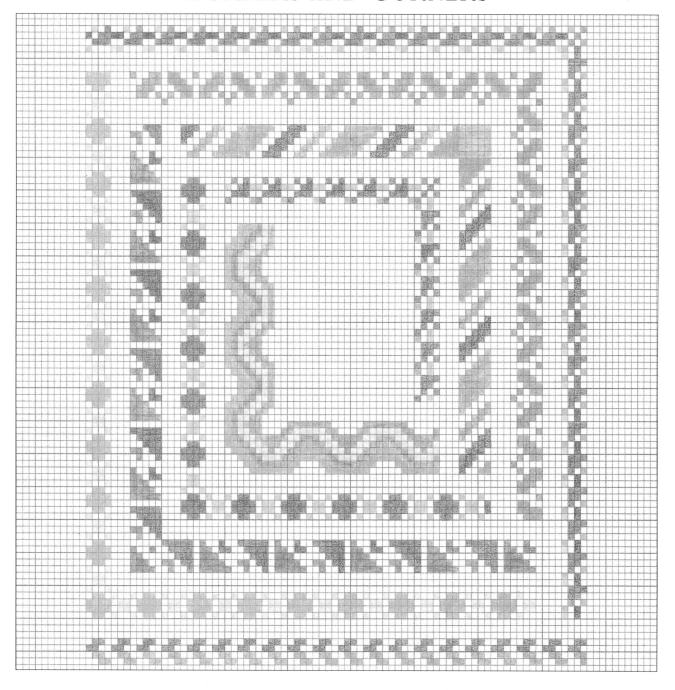

BORDERS AND CORNERS

GEOMETRIC MOTIFS

GEOMETRIC MOTIFS

GEOMETRIC REPEAT PATTERNS

GEOMETRIC REPEAT PATTERNS

CROSS STITCH FOR SPECIAL OCCASIONS

LIBERALITY LIES LESS
IN GIVING
THAN IN THE TIMELINESS
OF THE GIFT.

Les Caractères
JEAN DE LA BRUYÈRE

CHRISTENING GOWN

*A pretty first white dress is a useful and very acceptable gift for a new arrival. This dress has
the tiniest border of pink and yellow roses embroidered across the front yoke, a full skirt and
short puff sleeves. To complete the ensemble for a baptism, the little jacket on page 46,
would keep the baby snug and warm. Because of its simplicity as a christening gown,
it would just as easily double as a special occasion dress. The finished dress
measures 56 cm (22 in) around the chest and 64 cm (25 in) long.*

MATERIALS

- 33 x 23 cm (13 x 9 in) of 36 count fine white linen, for the front bodice
- Tacking thread
- Tapestry needle size 26
- Embroidery hoop (optional)
- DMC stranded cotton: see the thread list below
- Dressmaker's graph paper
- 1.3 m (50 in) of white lawn, 112 cm (44 in) wide
- Matching sewing thread
- Two white buttons, 6 mm (¼ in) across
- 1.7 m (1¼ yds) of pink ribbon, 12 mm (½ in) wide

THREAD LIST

445	pale lemon yellow	3354	light dusty pink
725	medium yellow	335	dark medium pink
783	golden brown	304	dark red
921	rust	524	sage green
818	baby pink	3012	light olive green

WORKING THE EMBROIDERY

1 Mark the vertical centre line of the linen with tacking stitches and then mark the horizontal positioning line about 8 cm (3 in) in from the bottom edge. Place the linen in an embroidery hoop (see page 132) or work in the hand, as you prefer.

2 Following the colour key and the chart given on page 98, where one square represents three threads of fabric, work the embroidery outwards from the middle, using two strands of thread in the needle. Leaving the tacking stitches in place, lightly steam-press the embroidery on the wrong side.

FINISHING

1 Enlarge the pattern pieces on page 99 onto dressmaker's graph paper (see page 133). Seam allowances of 1 cm (⅜ in) are included. Transfer all construction marks, then cut out.

2 Following the cutting layout on page 99, place the pattern pieces on the straight grain of the white lawn and cut out as instructed. Cut the neckband on the bias grain, as indicated in the diagram.

3 For the front bodice, align the tacking stitches on the linen with the dashed lines on the pattern before cutting out.

4 Machine-stitch the skirt, side seams together, using small French seams (see page 138). Machine-stitch the front and back bodices together at the sides in the same way.

5 On the skirt front, run a double row of gathering stitches between the points marked, and gently pull up the gathers to fit the bottom edge of the front bodice.

6 Fold the skirt back in half and cut an 18 cm (7 in) opening down the centre back. Gather the two top edges, at each side of the opening, and fit them to the two back bodice sections as for the front. With right sides together, pin and machine-stitch the front and back bodice to the skirt. Press the seams upwards.

7 With right sides together, stitch the shoulder seams and press them open.

8 To neaten the back opening, pin the facing in place with right sides together and machine-stitch, pivoting the needle at the lower point of the opening before returning along the second side. Make a single turning on

the facing, fold it to the wrong side of the opening and hem by hand, carefully stitching into the previously made stitches. Press.

9 Bind the neck edge with bias strip in the same way, hand-stitching it on the inside.

10 With right sides together, join the underarm seam on each sleeve and press open. Gather the bottom edge of the sleeve and apply the sleeve band as for the neck, first joining the band into a circle. Gather both sleeve heads and, with right sides together, pin them into the armholes, matching the sleeve seams to the side seams.

11 To close the dress, make two vertical buttonholes, 8 mm (⅜ in) long: one placed just below the neck binding and the second just above the bodice seam (see page 137 for making buttonholes). Sew on the buttons to correspond.

12 For the hem, make a single 1 cm (⅜ in) turning and then a 6 cm (2¼ in) turning. Pin and slipstitch in place. Lightly press. Using a single strand each of pink (3354) and yellow (725), work two rows of running stitches around the hem and neck edge to finish.

13 Stitch ribbon around the dress just above the bodice/skirt seam, using tiny slipstitches along both sides. Cut an 8 cm (3 in) length and make a tiny bow, folding in the ends and wrapping another small piece over them; stitch at the back. Cut the remaining ribbon in half and attach long tails to the centre front; cover the ends with the bow and then stitch through all layers to secure.

BELOW: *Each coloured square on the chart represents one cross stitch worked over three threads of fabric.*

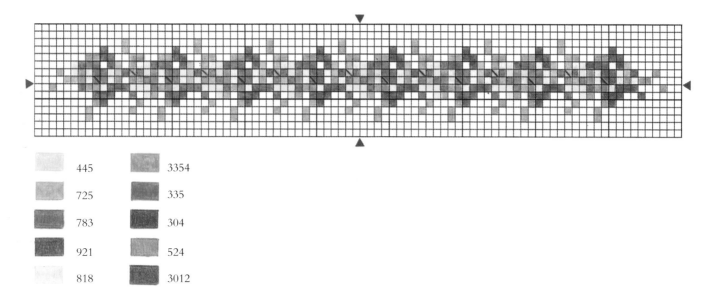

445		3354	
725		335	
783		304	
921		524	
818		3012	

112 cm (44 in) wide

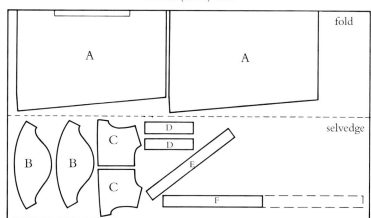

Cutting layout
A skirt
B sleeve
C back bodice
D sleeve band
E neck binding
F back opening facing

Each square = 2.5 cm (1 in)

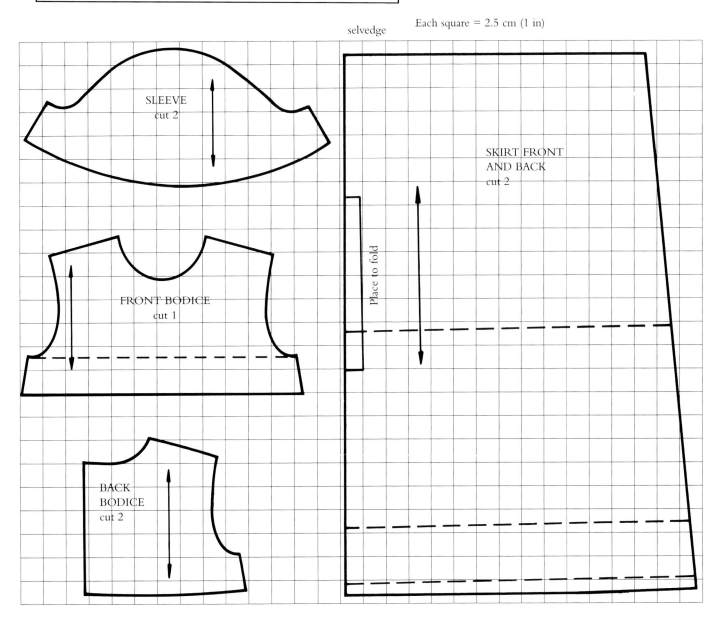

HEART-SHAPED PILLOW

The delightful custom of giving red roses to a loved one on St. Valentine's Day was the inspiration for this simple heart-shaped pillow. The giving of red roses during courtship is thought to have been started by Louis XVI of France who gave them to his queen, Marie Antoinette. A gift such as this pillow might be exchanged between sisters, mother and daughter or friends, for example, as a token of their love and friendship for each other. You could even fill it with sweet-smelling herbs to make it extra special. The finished pillow measures 18 x 15 cm (7 x 6 in).

MATERIALS

- 23 cm (9 in) square 16 count pale blue Aida fabric
- Tacking thread
- Tapestry needle size 26
- Embroidery hoop (optional)
- DMC stranded cotton: see the thread list below
- Tracing paper
- 23 cm (9 in) square of pale blue lining fabric
- 60 cm (24 in) of floral trim, 12 mm (½ in) wide
- Matching sewing threads
- Loose wadding for filling pillow
- 1 m (40 in) of two-colour contrast cord

THREAD LIST

743	yellow	580	deep olive green
472	light moss green	818	baby pink
3766	turquoise	605	pale magenta
907	lime green	603	medium magenta
733	medium olive green	601	magenta

WORKING THE EMBROIDERY

1 Mark the centre of the Aida fabric both ways with tacking stitches. Work in a hoop or in the hand as preferred (see page 132).

2 Following the colour key and the chart given on page 102, where each square represents one stitch worked over one intersection of fabric, start the embroidery in the centre. Use two strands of thread in the needle throughout and complete the cross stitching, working outwards from the middle.

3 Add the backstitching details to finish. Lightly press on the wrong side, if needed.

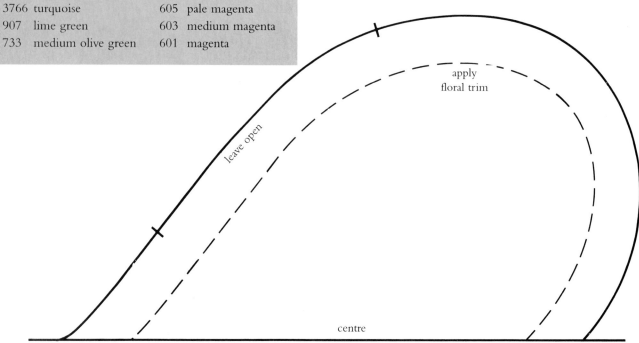

100

FINISHING

1 Trace the outline given opposite for the heart and draw the second half in reverse. Cut out the template. Pin the tracing on top of the embroidery, matching the centre line with the tacking stitches. Allow an extra 12 mm (½ in) seam allowance all round and cut out. Cut out the lining fabric to the same size.

2 Stitch the floral trim to the pillow front about 12 mm (½ in) in from the seamline, using matching thread and small running stitches, making tiny stitches on the right side and larger stitches on the wrong side.

3 With the right sides inside, pin the two sections together and machine stitch around the edge leaving a small opening in one side, as shown on the trace pattern. Trim the seam, clip into the curves and the inner angle before turning through to the right side.

4 Stuff with loose wadding to a softly rounded shape. You could also add some scented herbs or petals here, if you wish. Slipstitch the opening closed.

5 Cut a 20 cm (8 in) length of cord for the loop, fold in half and slip the ends into the seam at the top of the heart, first snipping the stitches to make a small opening. Slipstitch the cord around the edge of the pillow with matching thread, alternately catching the underside of the cord and sliding the needle under a few threads of the seam so that the finished stitching is completely hidden. Secure the ends and the opening with a few well-hidden stitches.

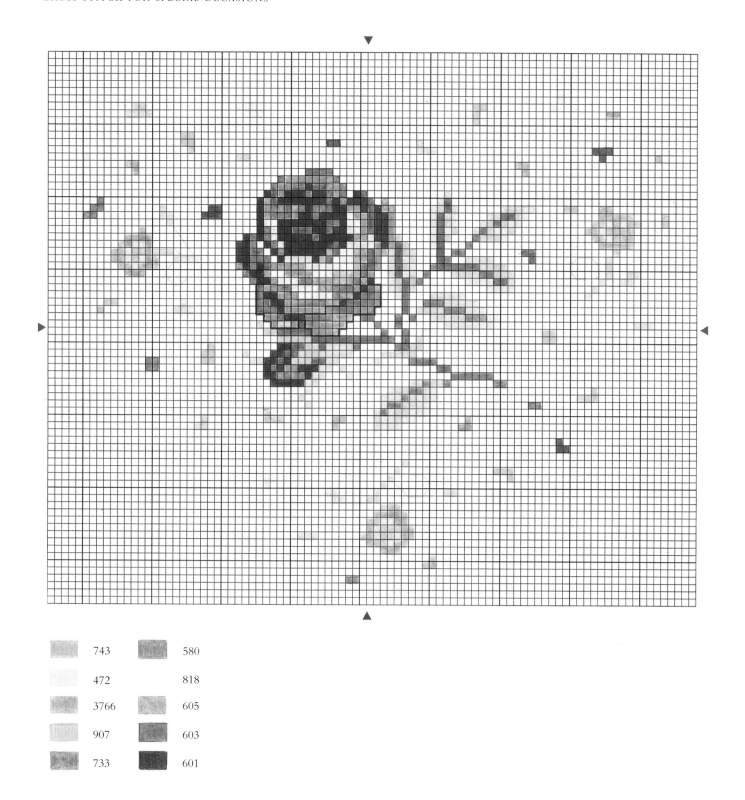

	743		580
	472		818
	3766		605
	907		603
	733		601

ABOVE: *Each coloured square represents one cross stitch worked over one intersection of fabric.*

EASTER GREETINGS CARD

The giving of eggs at Easter time is an old custom – they were originally given in Spring-time as a symbol of fertility, birth and growth but later became synonymous with the Resurrection of Christ. All kinds of eggs, ranging from dyed and painted birds' eggs to those carved from wood or made from chocolate, are still exchanged between families and friends around the world. What better way to celebrate Easter than to send your greetings with a pretty card in the shape of an egg that you have embroidered yourself? The finished greetings card measures overall 20 x 14 cm (8 x 5½ in) with a cut-out measuring 14 x 9.5 cm (5½ x 3¾ in).

MATERIALS

- 23 x 18 cm (9 x 7 in) of 14 count white Aida fabric
- Tacking thread
- Tapestry needle size 24
- Embroidery hoop (optional)
- DMC stranded cotton: see the thread list below
- Card mount with an oval cut-out

THREAD LIST

744	soft yellow	794	light dusty blue
729	old gold	799	medium soft blue
747	palest turquoise	818	baby pink
597	dusty turquoise	3354	light dusty pink
472	light moss green	3733	dusty pink
372	khaki	3350	dark dusty pink

WORKING THE EMBROIDERY

1 Mark the centre of the fabric both ways with tacking stitches. Work in a hoop or in the hand, as preferred (see page 132).

2 Following the colour key and the chart given on page 105, where each square represents one stitch worked over one intersection of fabric, begin the cross stitching in the centre. Use two strands of thread in the needle throughout and complete the embroidery, working outwards from the middle.

3 Finish by working the stems in backstitch using khaki (372), and then outline the bow with dusty turquoise (597). Similarly, outline the remaining ribbon and the picot edging.

FINISHING

1 Retain the tacking stitches as you will find them useful for centring the design in the card mount. Steam-press on the wrong side, taking care not to crush the stitching.

2 Open out the self-adhesive card mount and centrally place the embroidery over the cut-out area, using the tacking stitches as a guide. Trim the fabric so that it is 12 mm (½ in) bigger all round than the marked area on the card.

3 Take out the tacking stitches. Reposition the embroidery, fold over the left-hand section of the card and press firmly to secure.

ADAPTING THE EASTER GREETINGS CARD

Greetings cards are always welcome, whatever the time of year or occasion, and sending a card or even an invitation that you have embroidered yourself is a wonderfully personal touch. This book is full of designs that can easily be adapted to fit inside a card mount, so you should be able to find inspiration for birthday cards, Christmas cards, anniversary invitations ... the list is endless. Card mounts are widely available and come in many different shapes and sizes, so you are sure to find one that will suit your needs. The **Greetings Cards Pattern Library** on pages 106–107 provides you with small alphabets and Zodiac motifs which are sure to be useful when designing your own cards or invitations.

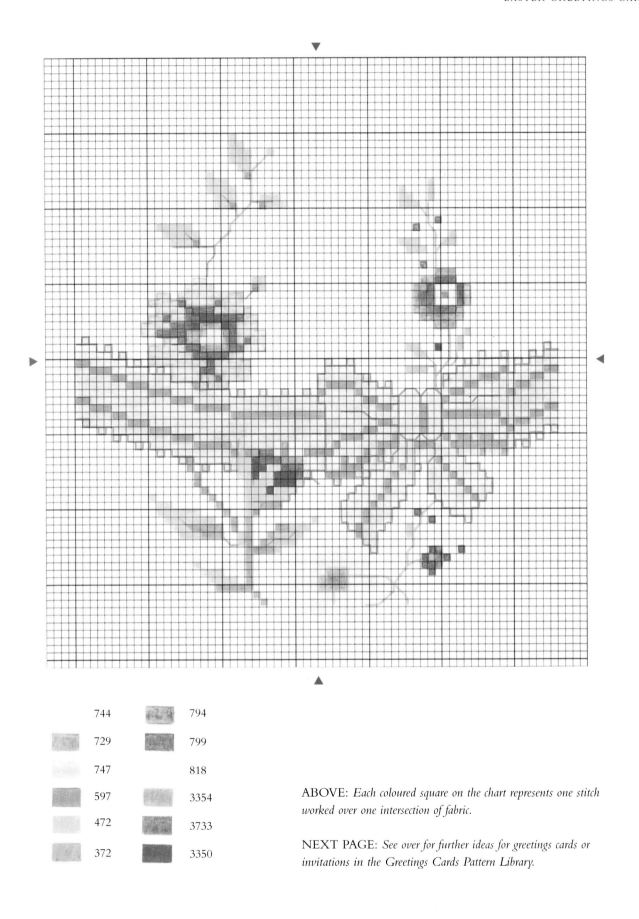

	744		794
	729		799
	747		818
	597		3354
	472		3733
	372		3350

ABOVE: *Each coloured square on the chart represents one stitch worked over one intersection of fabric.*

NEXT PAGE: *See over for further ideas for greetings cards or invitations in the Greetings Cards Pattern Library.*

SMALL ALPHABETS FOR GREETINGS CARDS

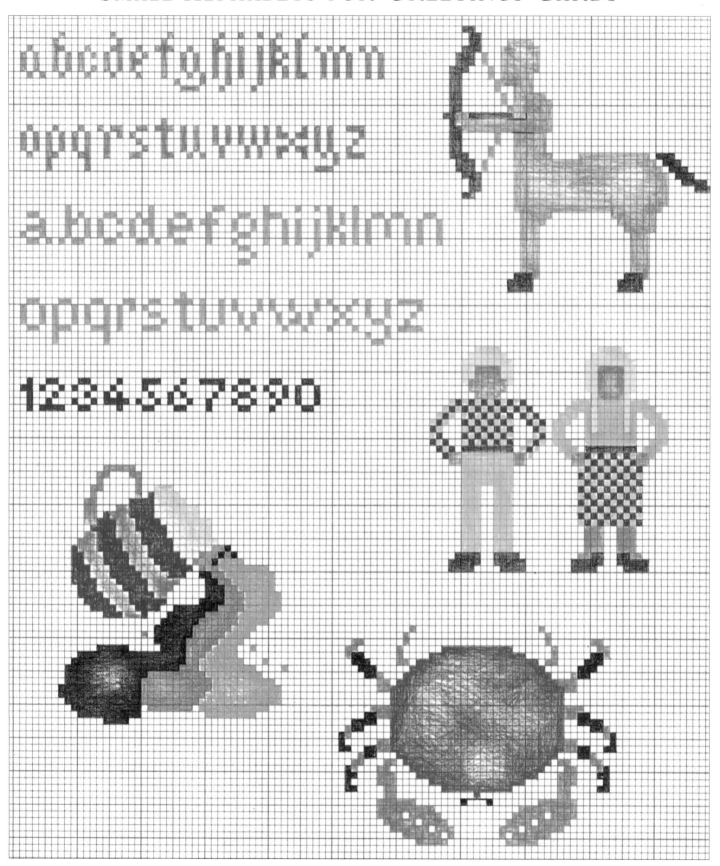

ZODIAC MOTIFS

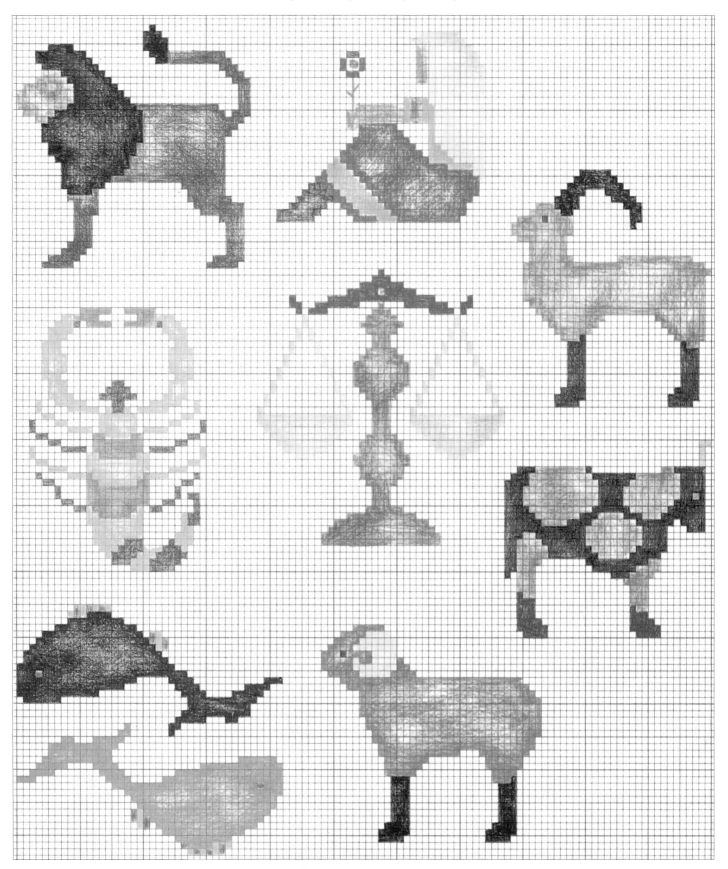

INITIALLED NAPKINS

Stitch a set of spotless white napkins and trim each of them with a decorated initial. Napkins are quick and simple to embroider, and a set bearing the appropriate initials would make a delightful present for family and friends alike. Why not bring them out to celebrate a special birthday dinner? If you have lots of time, napkins bearing both the bride's and groom's initials at a wedding, or both husband's and wife's initials at an anniversary dinner, are a wonderful detail.

MATERIALS

- 130 cm (51 in) wide 18 count white Aida evenweave fabric
- DMC stranded cotton: see the thread list below
- Tapestry needle size 24
- Tacking thread in a dark colour
- Matching sewing thread
- Sewing needle and pins
- Small embroidery hoop

THREAD LIST

603	medium magenta	699	dark leaf green
552	medium purple	906	vivid green
995	deep kingfisher blue		

PREPARING THE FABRIC

1 Napkins are usually square, varying in size from small tea napkins of 30 cm (12 in) to large dinner napkins of 60 cm (24 in). Decide on a size which will suit your requirements, adding 2 cm (³⁄₄ in) all round for the hem allowance. When using this type of evenweave fabric a good all-purpose size is 38 cm (15 in) square. Lengths of 130 cm (51 in) wide fabric can be divided evenly into three for napkins of this size with sufficient left for hem allowances after trimming away the selvedges. From a 90 cm (36 in) length of fabric, you will be able to cut a set of six napkins.

2 Cut the fabric into pieces of the required size and mark the position of each initial with vertical and horizontal lines of tacking stitches. Keep the initial about 6 cm (2¼ in) from the finished edges on two adjacent sides of the napkin.

ABOVE: *Make a set of initialled napkins, choosing thread colours to co-ordinate with your tableware. You may prefer to work a simpler initial for everyday napkins. Choose one from the selection shown in the alphabet pattern library (pages 123-127).*

WORKING THE EMBROIDERY

1 Mount the corner of the fabric in the embroidery hoop (see page 132).

2 Begin stitching at the edge of the tacked rectangle. Work in cross stitch from the chart, using three strands of thread in the needle throughout. Each square on the chart represents one cross stitch worked over two vertical and two horizontal woven blocks of fabric.

FINISHING

1 Press the embroidery carefully on the wrong side with a warm iron, pressing down lightly and taking care not to crush the stitches.

2 Pin and tack a narrow double hem (see page 136) round the edge, turning in the corners neatly. Secure the hem with hemming stitch worked by hand (see page 136), or a row of machine stitching.

RIGHT: *Each coloured square represents one stitch worked over two vertical and two horizontal woven blocks of fabric.*

FAR RIGHT: *The chart shown on the far right shows the letter 'A' decorated with two tiny flower and leaf motifs. Use these motifs to decorate the other letters of the alphabet.*

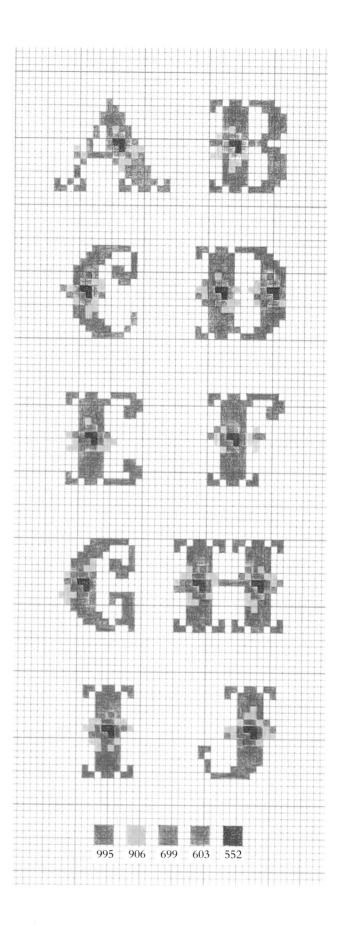

995 906 699 603 552

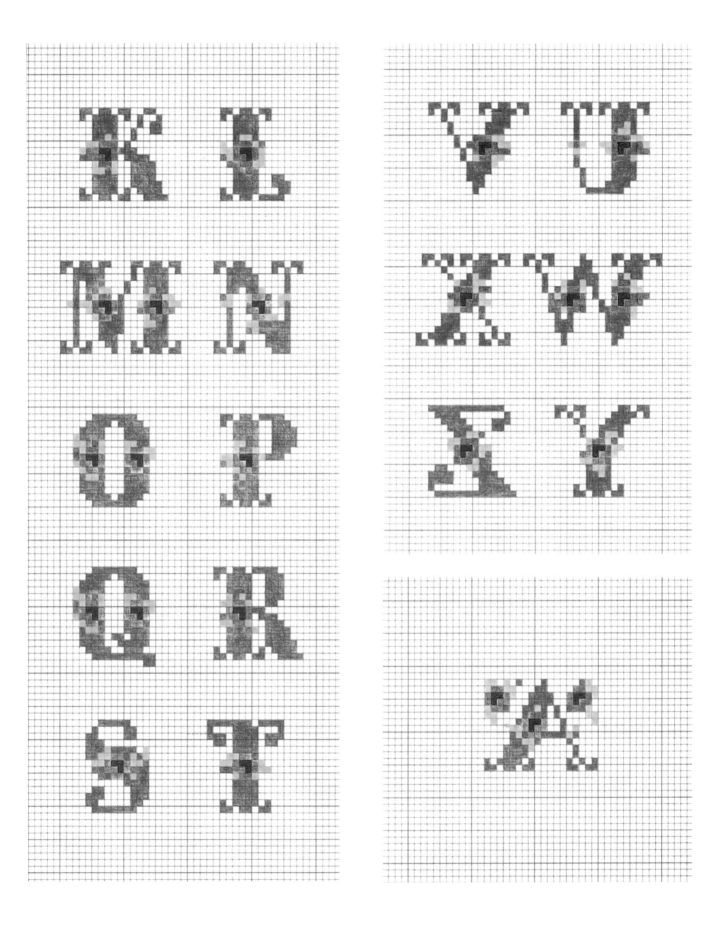

CHRISTMAS TREE
ORNAMENTS

*Long before shiny baubles and tinsel were invented, it was customary to decorate the
Christmas tree with handmade ornaments and toys. These would include small toys – as
well as simple biscuits and sweetmeats carefully moulded and placed in pretty baskets or
containers of some kind. Preparing for Christmas is always exciting, and decorating the tree
is a special event in most households. Each year we unwrap our treasured heirlooms and add
new decorations to our collection. You could add one or two of the cross-stitched ornaments to
an existing collection or begin a new one using just one of the motifs, such as the star or
sweetie-filled cone decorated with a cupid, for example. Children love them!*

STAR

The finished star measures
10 x 10 cm (4 x 4 in)

MATERIALS
- Two 15 cm (6 in) squares of 14 count white
  Aida fabric
- Tacking thread
- Tapestry needle size 24
- Small embroidery hoop (optional)
- DMC stranded cotton: see the thread list below
- Tracing paper
- Two 10 cm (4 in) squares of thin cardboard
- Two 10 cm (4 in) squares of lightweight wadding
- Masking tape
- 80 cm (31 in) of 3 mm (½ in) wide red ribbon
- Fabric glue
- One red bead, 1 cm (⅜ in) across

THREAD LIST
666 bright red

SNOWMAN

The finished snowman measures
13 x 8 cm (5 x 3 in)

MATERIALS
- Two 18 x 13 cm (7 x 5 in) pieces of 14 count
  white Aida fabric
- Tacking thread
- Tapestry needle size 24
- Small embroidery hoop (optional)
- DMC stranded cotton: see the thread list below
- Tracing paper
- Two 13 x 8 cm (5 x 3 in) pieces of thin cardboard
- Two 13 x 8 cm (5 x 3 in) pieces of lightweight
  wadding
- Masking tape
- 80 cm (31 in) of 3 mm (⅛ in) wide light
  blue ribbon
- Fabric glue
- One blue bead, 1 cm (⅜ in) across

THREAD LIST
606 hot red	958 mint green
341 lavender blue	310 black

WORKING THE EMBROIDERY

1 All four ornaments are embroidered in the same way.
  Mark the centre of your fabric both ways with tacking
stitches. You can work in a hoop, but as long as you keep an
even tension, small amounts of embroidery can be worked
in the hand without risk of pulling the fabric out of shape.

2 Following the appropriate colour key and chart given
  on page 115, where each square represents one stitch

worked over one fabric block, work the cross stitch
outwards from the middle using two strands of thread in the
needle. Add the backstitching to finish.

3 For the angel ornament, attach the gold beads in the
  places indicated on the chart (see page 135 for
instructions on sewing on beads).

ANGEL
The finished angel measures
10 x 10 cm (4 x 4 in)

MATERIALS
- Two 15 cm (6 in) squares of 14 count white Aida fabric
- Tacking thread
- Tapestry needle size 24
- Small embroidery hoop (optional)
- Light gold metallic thread
- 27 tiny gold beads
- One white bead, 1 cm (³/₈ in) across
- Tracing paper
- Two 10 cm (4 in) squares of thin cardboard
- Two 10 cm (4 in) squares of lightweight wadding
- Masking tape
- 1 m (40 in) of 3 mm (¹/₈ in) wide gold ribbon or Russia braid
- Fabric glue
- One metallic bell, 1 cm (³/₈ in) across

THREAD LIST
DMC light gold metallic thread

FINISHING

STAR, SNOWMAN AND ANGEL

1 Transfer the outline given on page 116 to the card. Either trace it and place the tracing pencil side down on the card and go over the outline, or photocopy the page and cut out the shape which you can then place on the card, draw around and cut out. Using this as a template, cut out the two pieces of wadding.

2 Assemble the three layers: put the wadding on the card with the embroidery on top, right side up. Secure the fabric edges to the back of the card with masking tape. Cover the second piece of card in the same way. With the front and back sections together, overcast the edges. Cover the edge with the ribbon, attaching it with a thin coating of fabric glue. Apart from the angel, finish with a loop on top and then thread on a bead to cover the join. Knot above the bead to hold it in place (see right).

CONE WITH CUPID
The finished cone measures
14 x 9 cm (5½ x 3½ in)

MATERIALS
- 23 x 17 cm (9 x 6½ in) of 14 count green Aida fabric
- Tacking thread
- 23 x 17 cm (9 x 6½ in) of contrast cotton fabric for the lining
- DMC stranded cotton: see the thread list below
- Tapestry needle size 24
- Contrasting bias binding, 12 mm (½ in) wide
- Matching sewing thread

THREAD LIST
225	palest damson pink	3756	pale powder blue
754	medium flesh pink	928	light grey green
676	buff	351	pale red
742	light orange	988	grass green
959	light mint green		

3 For the angel, begin sticking on the gold ribbon at the centre bottom edge, leaving a tail of about 8 cm (3 in). Continue as before, finishing at the centre bottom and leaving a matching tail. At the top, stitch the two ribbons together to form a loop and attach the bell with a knot to the bottom.

CONE WITH CUPID

1 Trace the quarter circle on page 116, add a 1 cm (³/₈ in) seam allowance to both straight edges, and cut out.

2 Place the pattern on your embroidery with the centre lines matching, and cut out. Cut out the lining fabric to the same shape. Put the two fabrics wrong sides together and treat as one. Cover the curved edge with bias binding (see page 139).

3 With the right side inside, place the two straight edges together and machine-stitch to secure. Trim the seam back to 6 mm (¼ in) and zigzag stitch the raw edge to neaten. Turn through to the right side.

4 To make a hanging loop from bias binding, cut a length of about 30 cm (12 in) and stitch the two folded edges together. Turn under the short edges and attach to the cone, covering the seam with one end and placing the other at the opposite side. Hem in place with matching thread.

STAR

SNOWMAN

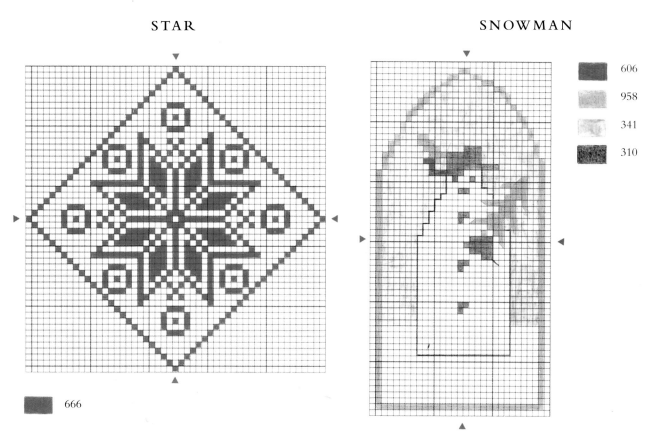

	606
	958
	341
	310

	666

ANGEL

CONE WITH CUPID

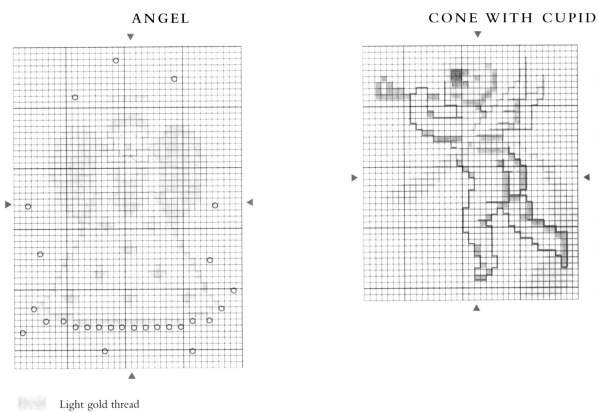

	225
	754
	676
	742
	959
	3756
	928
	351
	988

	Light gold thread
O	Gold beads

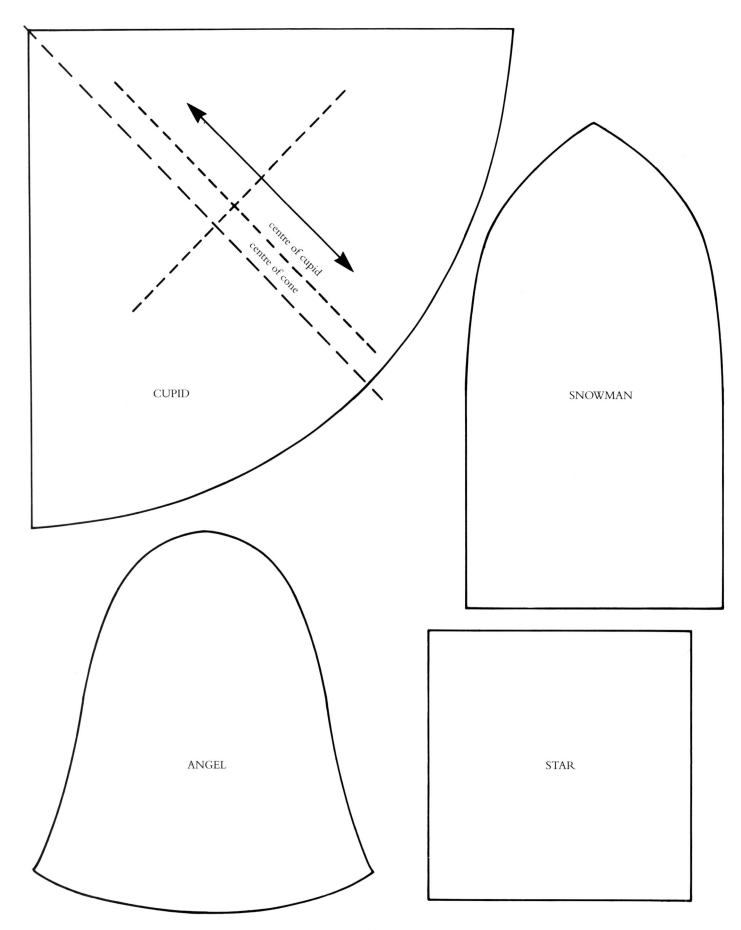

centre of cupid

centre of cone

CUPID

SNOWMAN

ANGEL

STAR

CHRISTMAS STOCKINGS

The delightful custom of children hanging up a stocking on Christmas Eve ready for Father Christmas's arrival is thought to have begun with the story of Saint Nicholas. Legend tells how a father was unable to provide dowries for his three daughters so, one night, Saint Nicholas threw purses of gold through the house window and they were caught in stockings which had been left to dry by the fire. Today, we like to fill our children's stockings with lots of small gifts, aiming to keep them occupied until larger gifts are opened later in the day. You may wish to work the recipient's name or initials into the design so the child will always have his or her own very special stocking ready at Christmas time. The finished stockings measure 30 x 13 cm (12 x 5 in).

MATERIALS
FOR EACH STOCKING

- 18 x 10 cm (7 x 4 in) of 18 count white Aida fabric
- Tacking thread
- Tapestry needle size 26
- Small embroidery hoop (optional)
- DMC stranded cotton: see the thread list below
- Dressmaker's graph paper
- 38 cm (15 in) square of contrast cotton fabric for the lining
- 38 cm (15 in) square of lightweight synthetic wadding

REINDEER STOCKING

- 38 cm (15 in) square of green cotton fabric
- Red cotton bias binding, 12 mm (½ in) wide

NOEL STOCKING

- 38 cm (15 in) square of red cotton fabric
- Green cotton bias binding, 12 mm (½ in) wide

THREAD LIST

606	hot red	B5200	white
992	medium blue green		

WORKING THE EMBROIDERY

1 Both stockings are embroidered and made in the same way. Mark the centre of the Aida fabric both ways with tacking stitches. Work in a small hoop or in the hand, as preferred (see page 132).

2 Following the colour key and the appropriate chart given on page 119, where each square represents one stitch worked over one intersection of fabric, begin the embroidery in the centre, using two strands of thread in the needle. Complete the cross stitching and outline the reindeer and stars in backstitch using red (606) thread. Remove the tacking stitches and lightly steam-press on the wrong side.

FINISHING

1 Enlarge the stocking pattern pieces given on page 119 onto dressmaker's graph paper (see page 133) and cut out the two pattern pieces as instructed in the diagram (page 119). Cut out the stocking from red or green fabric. Using the back stocking pattern piece, cut out two pieces from the lining fabric and two from the wadding and put them to one side.

2 Trim the edges of the embroidered front band to measure 15 x 8.5 cm (6 x 3¼ in). Cover the bottom edge with bias binding (see page 139). Join the band to the front stocking section: with both pieces right side up, pin the band over the top raw edge of the stocking and machine-stitch across through the edge of the binding.

3 Assemble the layers for the two stocking sections as follows: place the lining wrong side up, the wadding next and then the top fabric right side up: trim the top band to size, shaping the sides outwards. Pin the layers together and, using white (B5200) stranded cotton (six strands), work large French knots (see page 135) at random over the surface to hold the layers secure. Tack around the edges of both pieces. Cover the top edge of both sections with bias binding.

4 Place the two pieces together, right sides out, then pin and tack around the edge. Cover the raw edges with bias binding. To make a loop at the top edge, extend the binding by about 13 cm (5 in) and machine-stitch the edges together along with the final stitching. Fold into a loop and hand-stitch to the top inside edge.

RIGHT: *Each coloured square on the charts represents one cross stitch worked over one intersection of fabric.*
BELOW: *These delightful Christmas stockings will bring much joy to children, especially when brimful with gifts. As an alternative you could stitch different motifs to the ones given here, drawing your inspiration from the Christmas Pattern Library on page 122.*

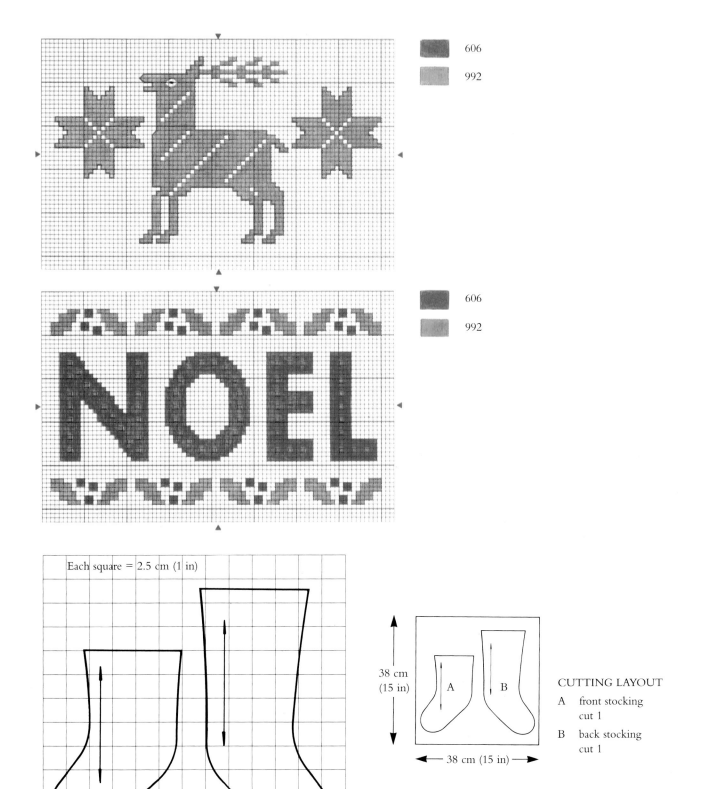

606

992

606

992

Each square = 2.5 cm (1 in)

38 cm
(15 in)

A

B

← 38 cm (15 in) →

CUTTING LAYOUT

A   front stocking
    cut 1

B   back stocking
    cut 1

CHRISTMAS HEIRLOOM

Make this German-style Advent calendar to celebrate the coming of Christmas. There is a tiny, gift-wrapped parcel or chocolate decoration to unwrap every day during December until Christmas Day finally arrives. To use the calendar in future years, bring it out of storage and add new gifts.

MATERIALS

- 110 cm (43 in) wide 11 count pale green Aida evenweave fabric
- DMC stranded cotton: see the thread list below
- Narrow green and red satin ribbon
- Empty matchboxes or other small boxes
- Small gifts
- Wrapped chocolate Christmas decorations
- 24 small brass curtain or tie-back rings
- Metallic Christmas wrapping paper
- Tapestry needle size 24
- Tacking thread in a dark colour
- Bright red sewing thread
- Sewing needle and pins
- Adjustable rectangular embroidery frame or large embroidery hoop
- Sturdy cardboard
- Strong linen carpet thread or very fine string

THREAD LIST

335	dark medium pink	996	kingfisher blue
208	purple	796	deep blue
666	bright red	3760	mid blue
947	deep orange	702	green
444	yellow	976	tan

PREPARING THE FABRIC

1 The embroidered area of the Advent calendar measures approximately 38 x 55 cm (15 x 21³/₄ in), but you will need to add at least 20 cm (8 in) all round to allow for mounting the fabric in a frame to work the stitching and so that the finished embroidery can be laced round card prior to framing.

2 Cut out the fabric to the required size. Using the photograph as a guide, scatter the gifts randomly across the fabric, marking the position of each one with a pin.

When you are happy with the arrangement, mark the position of each number above a gift with rows of tacking, making sure you include every number from 1 to 24. Remove the gifts and the pins. Mount the fabric in the embroidery frame or hoop (see pages 132-133).

WORKING THE EMBROIDERY

1 Stitch each number individually in cross stitch (page 134). Each coloured square on the chart represents one complete stitch worked over one woven block of fabric. Use three strands of thread in the needle throughout.

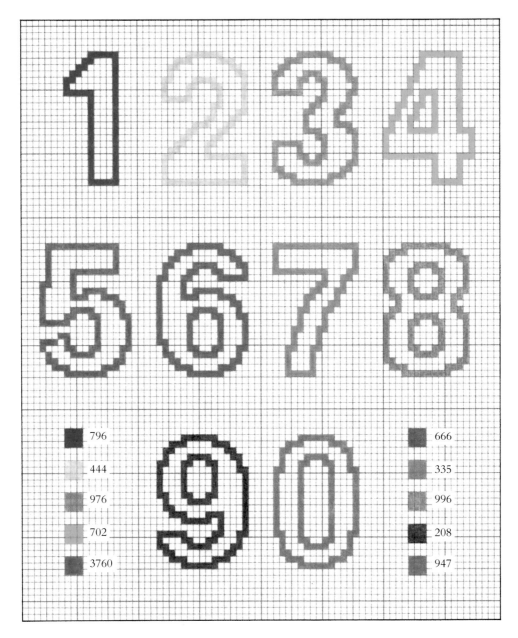

796
444
976
702
3760

666
335
996
208
947

2 Work carefully from the chart, stopping at intervals to check that the individual components are spaced correctly and that the top diagonal of each stitch faces in the same direction.

3 Outline each number (except those stitched in deep blue) with a row of back stitch (page 134) using two strands of deep blue (796) in the needle.

FINISHING

1 Using a warm iron, press the embroidery very lightly on the wrong side over a well-padded surface.

2 Using red sewing thread, attach a ring below each number. Lace the embroidery (page 141) securely over a piece of sturdy card cut to the appropriate size. Use strong linen carpet thread or very fine string for the lacing. Frame your work, following the suggestions given on page 141.

3 Place the gifts in the boxes, wrap them with paper and tie them with ribbon. Finally, attach a wrapped gift or chocolate decoration to each ring.

NEXT PAGE: *For further inspiration, the* **Christmas Pattern Library** *overleaf has designs for different motifs and patterns that could be embroidered on calendars, cards, stockings or other Christmas decorations.*

CHRISTMAS PATTERN LIBRARY

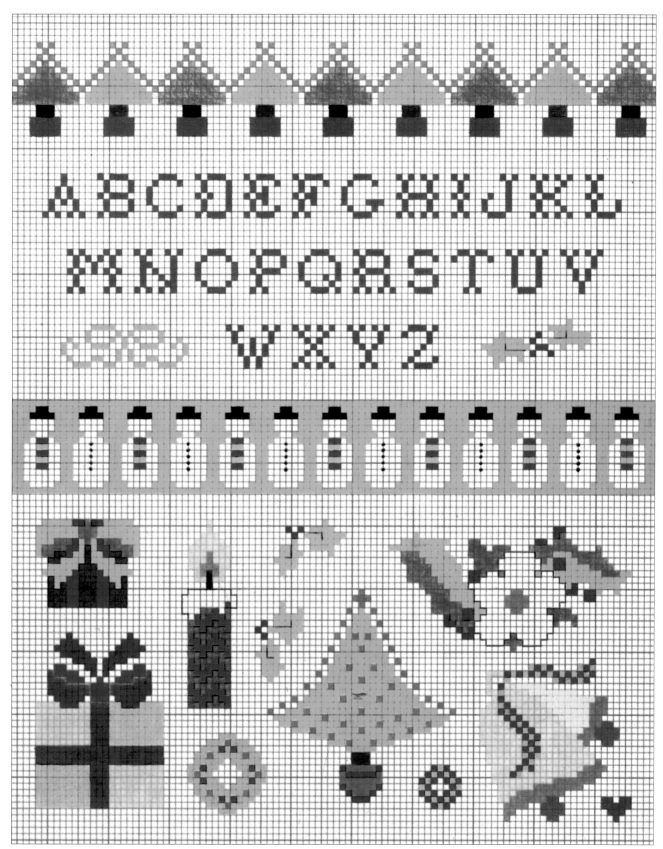

ALPHABET PATTERN LIBRARY

Take inspiration from the alphabets on the following pages to add monograms or decorative wording to your cross stitch embroideries. Monograms are a great way to personalize your work or draw attention to the fact that your creations are handmade.

ALPHABET PATTERN LIBRARY

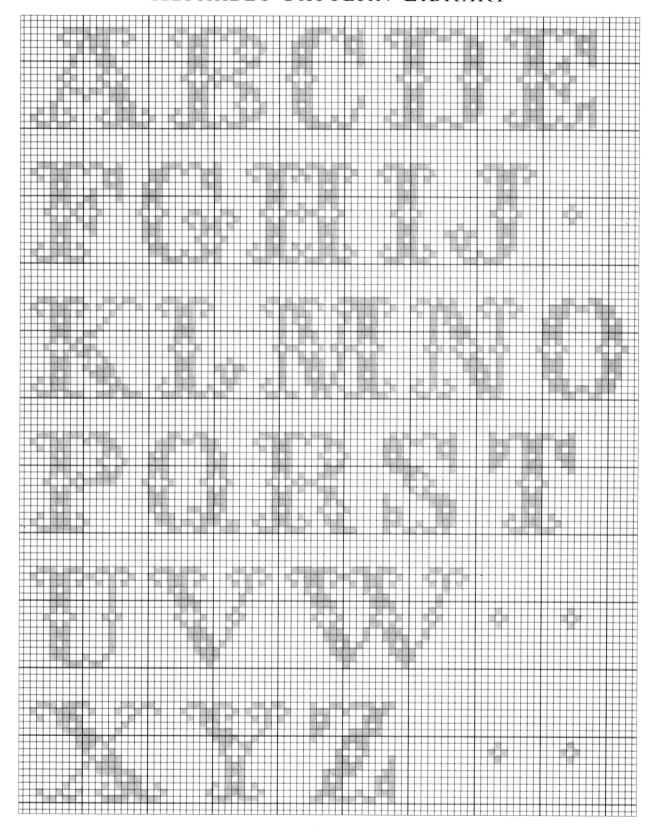

ALPHABET PATTERN LIBRARY

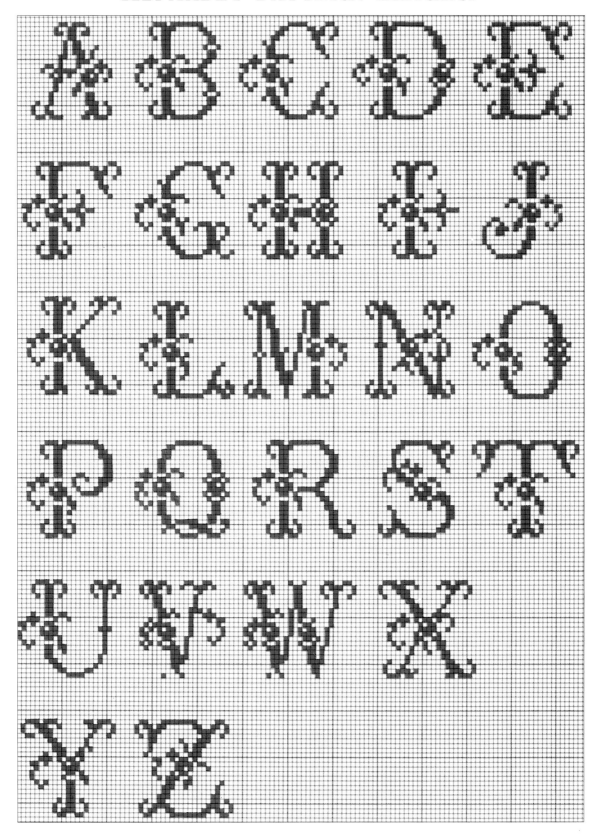

ALPHABET PATTERN LIBRARY

ALPHABET PATTERN LIBRARY

MATERIALS
AND SKILLS

MATERIALS AND SKILLS

The next few pages will provide you with information and help, designed to make your embroidery easier to stitch and look even better when finished. All the basic materials for cross stitch are discussed here, together with fully illustrated techniques for every embroidery stitch and finish that is used in the projects in this book. Each project makes cross-references to this section at the relevant points, but it would be equally valuable to read this section before beginning to sew.

FABRICS

Cross stitch embroidery is best worked on an evenweave fabric – that is, any fabric with the same number of threads counted in both directions, usually over 2.5 cm (1 in). The fabric is sometimes referred to as 14, 18 or 24 count, for example.

Linens are traditionally used for cross stitch embroidery around the world. They are available in a range of 'counts' and colours, although natural and antique finishes are more traditional. Some linens may have a pronounced uneven appearance – due to the staple (fibre) and nature of the flax from which it is woven – but this is what gives linen its distinguishing hand-made look.

Most linens are woven with a single weave with the exception of Hardanger, which has a double weave, and huckaback, which is woven in groups of threads (similar to cotton Aida) and forms a checked pattern.

In addition to linens, evenweave fabrics are also made from cotton and linen mixes, such as Zweigart's Quaker

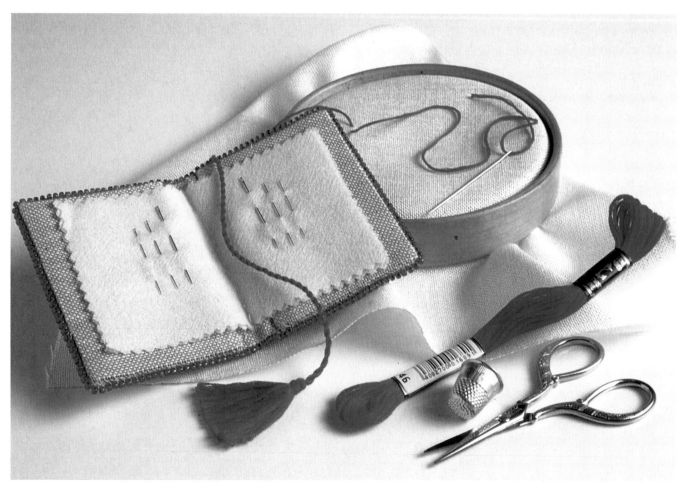

Cloth; pure cotton, such as Zweigart's Aida; and cotton and rayon mixes, such as Zweigart's Lugana. These names signify the different counts and all these fabrics come in a variety of colours.

The dressing given to these cotton fabrics may make them feel stiff and unyielding. On the one hand, the stiffness can help you to keep an even tension while stitching and will wash out with laundering but, on the other hand, you may prefer to hand-wash the fabric before starting.

The list of materials required, which is given with each project, states the types of fabrics you will need. Note that because some evenweave fabrics fray easily, an extra 3 cm (1¼ in) all round is sometimes included to allow for handling and stretching in a frame. For some of the larger projects you will need to measure up and calculate your own fabric requirements.

THREADS

Embroidery threads: many types of embroidery thread can be used for cross stitch work, including pearl threads and *coton à broder*, but, for the projects given in this book, DMC six-stranded embroidery cotton has been used throughout. A separate list for DMC stranded embroidery cotton is given with each chart. For most of the projects you will need one skein of each colour. For the larger projects, estimate the amount of thread required by using one complete skein of each colour first and then measuring how much of the design is completed. Obviously, for small areas you will use less than a skein so it would be economical first to check if you already have oddments of the same colours that could be used. The exact number of strands used for each project is given with the instructions.

As a rule, fewer strands are used on finer fabrics and more strands on heavier fabrics. The overall aim, however, is to produce clearly defined stitches that cover the fabric well.

Tacking thread: tacking thread is a soft, loosely twisted cotton which is normally sold on large reels, and is cheaper to use than ordinary sewing thread. The advantages of using tacking thread are that it will not leave a mark when it has been pressed with an iron, whereas ordinary sewing thread often does. Should it get caught up in any way while you are removing the stitches, it will break first rather than damage the fabric.

Sewing threads: these threads are tightly twisted, fine and yet strong. The most popular varieties are made from cotton or cotton/polyester mixes and come in a huge variety of colours, so matching a ground fabric should not be difficult.

Once you have got your project threads together, it is a good idea to attach them to a piece of cardboard for safe keeping. You will need a piece of stiff cardboard with holes punched down one side. Cut your threads into a workable length of 50 cm (20 in) and knot them through the holes, adding their shade number opposite in the order of the thread list.

NEEDLES

Round-ended tapestry needles should be used for cross stitching on evenweave fabrics. You will find that they move easily between the fabric intersections without piercing the ground threads. Tapestry needles are available in sizes ranging from 18 to 26.

For making up the projects, you will also need a selection of Sharps needles for hand sewing.

For working additional surface embroidery you will sometimes need crewel needles. These needles have sharp points and long oval eyes and are available in sizes 1 to 10.

FRAMES

A hoop or rectangular frame will keep the fabric evenly stretched while stitching. While for smaller pieces of embroidery a frame is not essential, there are advantages to using one. When the fabric is supported in a frame, both hands are free to stitch – with one on top and one below, many people find they eventually stitch faster and more evenly this way.

SCISSORS

It is important to use the right type of scissors for the job. For cutting fabric, use sharp, dressmaker's shears. You will need small, sharp-pointed embroidery scissors for snipping into seams and neatening threads, and for cutting cardboard, cords and paper, a pair of general-purpose scissors.

SEWING MACHINE

A sewing machine is useful for making up items, especially for larger projects, where it will give a stronger seam and also help to speed up the finishing process.

GENERAL ACCESSORIES

In addition to the above-mentioned items, you will need stainless steel pins, a long ruler and pencil, a tape measure, an iron and ironing board, and a thimble for hand sewing, especially through bulky seams.

PREPARING THE FABRIC

Before cutting out, steam-press the fabric to remove all creases. Stubborn creases will be impossible to remove once they have been embroidered over so, if possible, avoid using that particular area of fabric. If coloured fabrics are chosen for items you wish to launder, they should first be washed and pressed to test for colourfastness.

Always try to cut your fabric as economically as possible, placing pattern pieces as shown in the cutting layouts with individual projects to avoid wasting fabric.

Many evenweave fabrics, such as linen, fray very easily in the hand so, before you begin, it is a good idea to overcast the edges using tacking thread.

WORKING IN A HOOP

The hoop is most popular for working relatively small areas of embroidery. A hoop consists of two rings, usually made from wood, which fit closely one inside the other. The outer ring has a screw attachment so that the tension of the fabric can be adjusted and held firmly in place while the fabric is embroidered.

Hoops are available in several sizes ranging from 10 cm (4 in) in diameter to very large quilting hoops measuring 60 cm (24 in) across. Hoops with table- or floor-stand attachments are also available.

Do not leave your embroidery in the hoop for any length of time, as it will mark the fabric and these pressure marks are very hard to remove. Always release the tension screw after you've finished stitching.

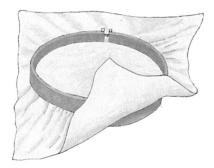

1 To stretch your fabric in a hoop, place the area to be embroidered right side up over the inner (smaller) ring and press the outer (larger) ring over it with the tension screw released.

2 Smooth the fabric and straighten the grain before tightening the tension screw attachment. The fabric should be evenly stretched.

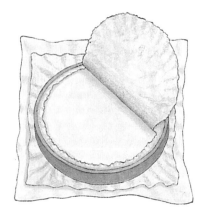

3 If wished, tissue paper can be placed between the outer ring and the embroidery, so that the hoop does not mark the fabric. Tear away the paper to reveal the fabric, as shown.

4 Alternatively, before stretching your fabric in the hoop, bind both rings with bias binding, essentially to stop the fabric from sagging or slipping (some fine linens can slip badly) and also to prevent the rings from leaving pressure marks on the fabric.

WORKING IN A RECTANGULAR FRAME

Rectangular frames are more popular for larger pieces of embroidery. They consist of two rollers with tapes attached, and two flat side pieces which slot into the rollers and are held in place by pegs or screw attachments.

These frames are measured by the length of the roller tape, and range in size from 30 cm (12 in) to 69 cm (27 in). They are also available with or without adjustable table- or floor-stands.

As an alternative to this kind of frame, canvas stretchers and old picture frames of an appropriate size can be used, and the fabric edges can simply be turned under and secured with drawing pins or staples.

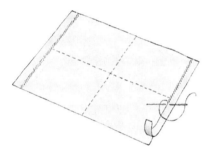

1 To stretch your fabric in a rectangular frame, cut out the fabric, allowing at least an extra 5 cm (2 in) all around the finished size of the embroidery. Tack a single 12 mm (½ in) turning on the top and bottom edges, and oversew 2.5 cm (1 in) wide tape to the other two sides. Mark the centre line both ways with tacking stitches.

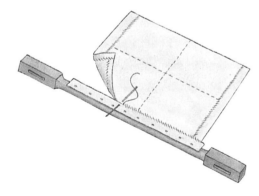

2 Working outwards from the centre, oversew the top and bottom edges to the roller tapes. Fit the side pieces into the slots, and roll any extra fabric onto one roller until it is taut.

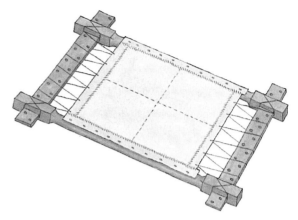

3 Insert the pegs or adjust the screw attachments to secure the frame. Thread a large-eyed needle (chenille needle) with strong thread and lace both edges, securing the ends by winding them around the intersections of the frame. Lace the webbing at 2.5 cm (1 in) intervals, stretching the fabric evenly.

ENLARGING A GRAPH PATTERN

There are one or two graph patterns given in the book which must first be enlarged to the correct size before you can use the pattern to cut out the fabric. The scale of the full-size pattern is given on the relevant page; for example, 'Each square = 5 cm (2 in)' means that each small square on the printed diagram corresponds to a 5 cm (2 in) square on your enlarged grid.

To enlarge a graph pattern, you will need a sheet of graph paper ruled in 1 cm (or 1 in) squares, a long ruler and pencil. If, for example, the scale is one square to 5 cm (2 in), you should first mark the appropriate lines to give a grid of the correct size. Copy the graph freehand from the small grid to the larger one, completing one square at a time. Use the ruler to draw the straight lines first, and then copy the curves freehand. Transfer all construction points and instructions before cutting out.

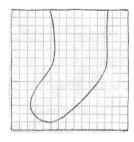

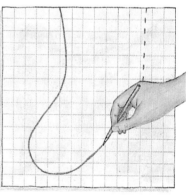

STARTING AND FINISHING

Never tie a knot at the end of the thread. A knot can show through the finished piece of work and make an unsightly lump on the right side. A knot may also come undone during laundering, resulting in your stitching unravelling. Instead, secure the thread by making one or two tiny stitches in a space that will be covered by embroidery. Alternatively, leave about 5 cm (2 in) of thread hanging loose which can be darned in later.

When working an area which is partly stitched, secure the new thread neatly on the wrong side by sliding the needle under a group of stitches to anchor about 2.5 cm (1 in) of thread underneath them. To finish a length of thread, slide the needle under a group of stitches on the wrong side and cut off the loose end.

CROSS STITCH

The following two methods of working are used for all cross stitch embroidery. In each case, neat rows of stitches are produced on the wrong side of the fabric.

1 Work in horizontal rows when stitching large solid areas. Working from right to left, complete the first row of evenly spaced diagonal stitches over the specific number of threads given in the project instructions. Then, working from left to right, repeat the process. Continue in this way, making sure that each stitch and successive rows cross in the same direction throughout the piece of embroidery.

2 When stitching diagonal lines, or individual groups of stitches, work downwards, completing each stitch before moving to the next.

BACKSTITCH

Backstitch is used in conjunction with cross stitch, sometimes for accompanying lettering but generally as an outline to emphasize a particular shape or shadow within a motif. The stitches are always worked over the same number of threads as the cross stitching to give uniformity to the finished embroidery. Use for continuous straight or diagonal lines.

Bring out the needle on the right side of the fabric and make the first stitch from left to right; pass the needle behind the fabric, and bring it out one stitch length ahead towards the left. Repeat and continue in this way along the stitchline.

RUNNING STITCH

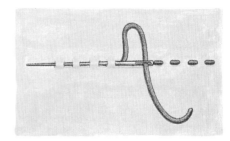

Working from right to left, take the needle in and out of the fabric at equal intervals, about 6 mm (¼ in) apart. Weave the needle in and out as many times as the fabric will permit before pulling the thread through.

BUTTONHOLE STITCH

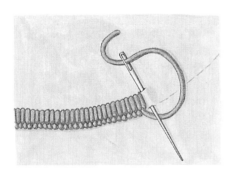

Bring the needle out on the stitchline. Working from left to right, insert the needle above the stitchline (the required depth of the stitch away) and just to the right. Then take a downward stitch and bring it out immediately below with the working thread under the needle. Tighten the loop and repeat to the end of the stitchline.

TYING A QUILTING KNOT

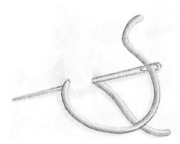

1 Working on the wrong side, make one stitch through all layers leaving a long end. Make a second stitch at the same point.

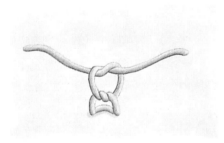

2 Tie the ends together, right over left, left over right. Do not pull too tightly. Trim the loose ends to 12 mm (½ in).

TO MAKE A FRENCH KNOT

Bring the needle out where the knot is to be worked and, holding the thread down with the left thumb, wind the thread twice round the needle.

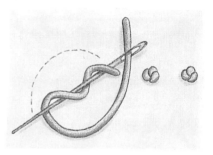

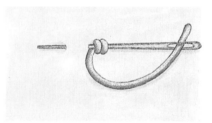

Insert the needle close to the starting point and pull it through to the back of the embroidery so that a knot forms on the right side of the fabric, then fasten off the thread. If making more than one knot, don't fasten off; instead, reposition the needle for the next knot.

STITCHING ON BEADS

Bring out the needle in the appropriate place and thread on a bead. Insert the needle into the same hole, make a stitch

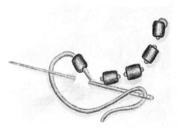

underneath (the length of the bead) and bring it out with the thread below the needle. Take the needle through to the back just beyond where it last emerged, then bring it out ready to attach the next bead.

HEMMING STITCH

This small, almost invisible stitch can be used for all types of hems and for finishing edges which have been covered with a fabric binding.

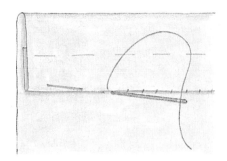

Fold the hem or binding to the wrong side and pin or tack to secure. Using matching thread and holding the needle at an angle, make a tiny stitch in the fabric first then insert it into the hem fold and make another small stitch. Pull the needle through and repeat along the stitchline, making the stitches of equal size and spacing them about 5 mm (¼ in) apart.

HEM-STITCH

This is a decorative way of turning up a hem and is the traditional stitch used on table linen and bed linen. For best results, hem-stitch should be worked on evenweave fabrics and fairly coarse weaves are the easiest to handle. Choose an embroidery thread similar in thickness to the threads of the fabric and use a tapestry needle to avoid piercing the fabric threads.

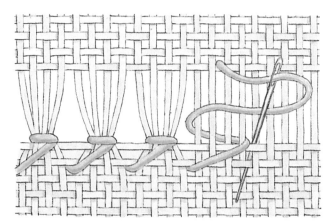

For a fringed finish, first remove a single thread at the hem and stitch along the line as shown. Complete the stitching and then remove the fabric threads below the hem-stitching to make the fringing.

To secure a hem that has been turned up to the drawn-thread line and tacked in place, work from the right side and hem-stitch as shown but, at the second stage of each stitch, make sure the needle pierces the hem at the back of the fabric before pulling the thread through ready to repeat the stitch along the line.

Bring the needle out on the right side of the fabric two threads below the drawn-thread line. Working from left to right, pick up either two or three threads, as shown in the diagram. Bring the needle out again and insert it behind the fabric, to emerge two threads down, ready to make the next stitch. Before reinserting the needle, pull the thread tight, so that the bound threads form a neat group.

Remember when hem-stitching Aida and other similar fabrics, that it is not necessary to remove the initial thread as the lines between the blocks of thread are clearly distinguished in the weaving. This means that the hem-stitching can easily be worked along a given line. As blocks and not single threads are being worked, make sure you refer to the project instructions for the number of blocks recommended for the hem-stitching.

SLIPSTITCH

This is a nearly invisible stitch formed by slipping the thread under a fold of fabric. It can be used to join two folded edges, such as a cushion opening, or one folded edge to a flat surface.

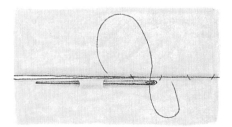

Working from right to left, bring the needle and thread out through one folded edge. For the first and each succeeding stitch, slip the needle through the fold of the opposite edge for about 6 mm (¼ in). Bring the needle out and continue to slip the needle alternately through the two folded edges.

VERTICAL BUTTONHOLE

For a handmade buttonhole, first mark the position with pins, placing it centrally within the hem of the opening.

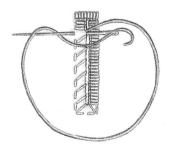

Using fine matching sewing thread, outline the shape of the buttonhole (a rectangle) with two rows of running stitches placed close together. Cut along the centre through all layers. Check that the button will easily pass through.

Working from left to right, insert the needle from behind the slit with the point downwards, and bring it out just below the running stitches. Pass the thread around the point of the needle, from right to left, pull the needle through in the opposite direction to place the purl stitch on the cut edge.

Complete one side of the buttonhole and then take several threads across the end of the slit. Buttonhole over them to make a small strengthening bar. Repeat on the opposite side to finish on the wrong side of the fabric.

MAKING A TASSEL

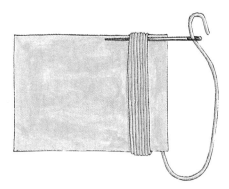

1 Make a very simple tassel by winding the appropriate embroidery or sewing thread around a small piece of card about 3 cm (1¼ in) wide. Thread the loose end into a needle, slip the tassel threads off the card and wind the loose thread several times round them, close to the top.

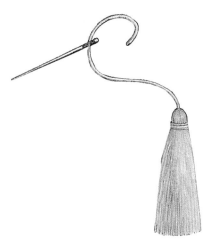

2 Pass the needle up through the bound threads and bring it out at the top of the tassel, ready to be sewn in place. Cut through the loops to finish.

STRAIGHT SEAMS

Unless otherwise stated, all seams are straight seams with a 1 cm (⅜ in) seam allowance, pressed open to finish. In some cases, a French seam may be specified while others are neatened by machine zigzag stitching.

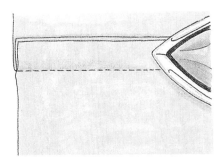

1 After stitching the seam, finish off the ends and steam-press the seam allowance to one side, to sink the stitches into the fabric.

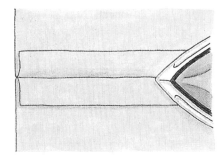

2 Press the seam allowances open, as shown. Remember to 'press as you sew' for best results when you are making up a project.

FRENCH SEAM

A French seam is stitched twice, once from the right side and once from the wrong side. On lightweight fabrics, it looks best if the finished width is 6 mm (¼ in) or less.

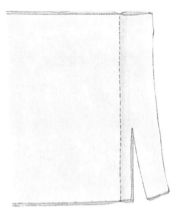

1 With the wrong sides of the fabric together, stitch 1 cm (⅜ in) from the edge. Trim the seam allowance to 3 mm (⅛ in) and press the seam open.

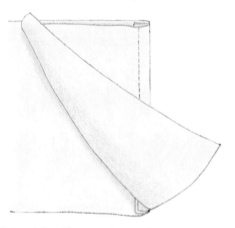

2 Fold the right sides together, with the stitched line exactly on the folded edge, and press again. Stitch on the seamline, which is now 6 mm (¼ in) from the fold. Press the seam to one side.

PIPED SEAMS

Contrasting piping adds a decorative finish to a seam and looks particularly attractive on items such as cushion covers. You can enclose pre-shunk piping cord with either bias cut fabric of your choice or with purchased bias binding. Alternatively, ready-covered piping cord is available in several widths and many colours. Also available are specially-made cord pipings which are applied in the same way.

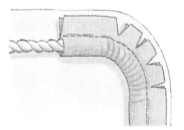

1 To apply piping, pin and tack it to the right side of the fabric, with the seamlines matching. Clip into curved seam allowances where necessary.

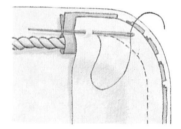

2 With the right sides together, place the second piece of fabric on top, enclosing the piping. Tack and then hand stitch in place. Alternatively, machine-stitch using the zipper foot. Stitch as close as possible to the piping, covering the first line of stitching.

3 To join the ends of piping cord together, first overlap the two ends by about 2.5 cm (1 in). Unpick the two cut ends of binding to reveal the cord. Join the binding strip as shown. Trim and press the seam open. Unravel and splice the two ends of cord, overstitching to secure them. Fold the bias binding over it, and finish stitching on the original stitchline.

ATTACHING DECORATIVE CORD

To attach a fine-to medium-weight cord, simply slip one cut end into the seam and leave a 2 cm (³⁄₄ in) gap in the seam and secure with matching thread. Slipstitch the cord around the edge of the cushion, alternately catching the underside of the cord and sliding the needle under a few threads of the seam so that the finished stitching is completely hidden.

Finish with the two ends neatly tucked into the seam; cross them smoothly and secure with a few well hidden stitches. Secure the seam opening in the same way.

BIAS BINDING

Bias binding is a narrow strip of fabric cut across the grain to allow maximum 'give', and is an excellent covering for all edges, especially curved ones. It is available in three sizes: 12 mm (½ in), 2.5 cm (1 in) and 5 cm (2 in), and in a wide range of colours. Cotton lawn is by far the most popular (and practical) type, and is stocked by most needlework suppliers.

These are two methods of binding an edge: one-stage binding, where the binding is attached by stitching through all layers, and two-stage binding, where it is attached in two stages so that the stitching cannot be seen on the right side.

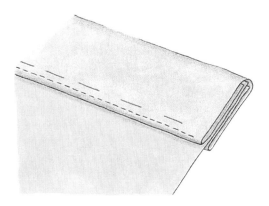

For one-stage binding, using double-folded binding, encase the raw edge with binding and tack in place. Working from the right side, machine-stitch along the edge, through all layers, so that both sides are stitched at the same time.

1 **For two-stage binding,** open out the turning on one edge of the binding and pin it in position on the fabric, right sides together, matching the foldline to the seamline. Fold over the cut end of the binding. Finish by overlapping the starting point by about 12 mm (½ in). Tack and machine-stitch along the seamline.

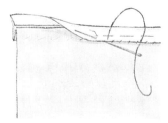

2 Fold the binding over the raw edge to the wrong side and tack in place. Then, using matching sewing thread, neatly hem to finish. Take the hemming stitch through the previously made stitches or place within the seam allowance to prevent them from showing on the right side.

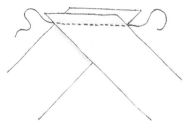

To join bias binding, cut the strips across the straight grain. Place them right sides together, pin and stitch across, and then press the seam open.

CUSHION TIES

Fabric ties, arranged singly or as a pair of bows, can be a decorative feature in themselves. Used to close a placket opening across the centre back of a cushion cover (as in the Blue and White Cushion project on page 24) the ties should be about 2.5 cm (1 in) wide and about 30 cm (12 in) long.

1 For medium weight fabrics, fold the fabric lengthways in half right sides facing, pin and machine stitch around two sides. Trim across the corners.

2 Using the blunt end of a knitting needle placed in the seam at the short end, turn the tie to the right side. Gradually ease the fabric over the end of the needle while pushing it through the fabric. Push out the corners and press the tie flat.

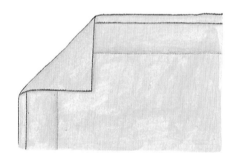

MITRING CORNERS

There are several types of mitre, but in each case the purpose is essentially to reduce bulk and to make the corner neat and square.

1 To mitre a corner, first plan the depth of the hem and allow an extra 6 mm (¼ in) for turning. Fold over the corner as shown in the diagram and finger-press the creaseline.

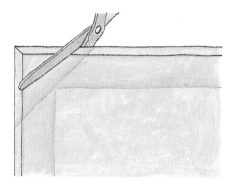

2 Allow a further 6 mm (¼ in) beyond this line and cut across.

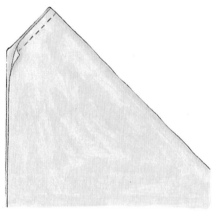

3 Fold the fabric with the two outer edges together and machine stitch across, taking a 6 mm (¼ in) seam and stopping at the creased line of the hem.

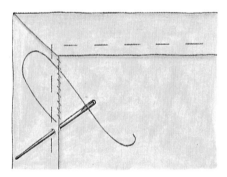

4 Press the seam open and turn the corner to the right side. Either turn under the hem, tack and hem on the wrong side, or finish the hem following the instructions given with the project.

MOUNTING EMBROIDERY

Embroidered pictures look best if they are first stretched over cardboard before framing under glass. A thin layer of wadding is placed between the fabric and the cardboard to give opaqueness and some protection to the corners and outer edges. Most fabrics used for cross stitch are fairly lightweight and can be attached at the back with pieces of masking tape, but heavier fabrics are best laced across the back with strong thread.

The cardboard should be cut to the size of the finished embroidery with, at least, an extra 6 mm (¼ in) added all around to allow for the recess in the picture frame.

Using a pencil, mark the centre both ways on the cardboard. Mark the centre of the wadding by placing pins in the middle of the outer edges. Lay the embroidery face down, centre the wadding on top and then the cardboard, aligning pencil marks, pins and tacking. Remove the pins.

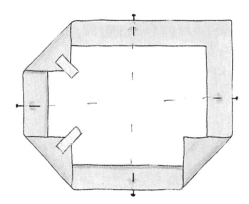

1 To attach the fabric with masking tape, begin by folding over the fabric at each corner and securing it with small pieces of masking tape.

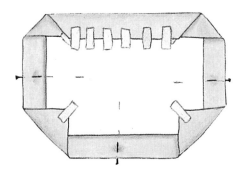

2 Working first on one side and then on the opposite side, fold over the fabric on all sides and secure it firmly with more pieces of masking tape, placed about 2.5 cm (1 in) apart. Check occasionally to see that the design is centred, and adjust the masking tape, if necessary. Neaten the mitred corners also with masking tape, pulling the fabric firmly to give a smooth even finish. Overstitch the mitred corners, if necessary.

To attach the fabric by lacing, lay the embroidery face down with the wadding and cardboard centred on top, as shown in the diagram. Begin with the corners, as shown,

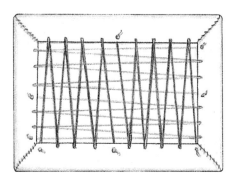

and also fold over the fabric on opposite sides, mitring the folds at the corners. Using strong thread knotted at one end and beginning in the middle of one side, lace across the two edges. Repeat on the other two sides. Finally, pull up the stitches fairly tightly to stretch the fabric evenly over the cardboard, periodically checking to see that your design is still centred. Adjust if necessary. Overstitch the mitred corners to finish.

FRAMING

There are several options available for framing your cross stitch creations. You can use a wooden stretcher, a simple clip frame or a conventional picture frame, with or without glass. Each of these methods has its disadvantages – for example, the stretcher method will not protect the embroidery from dust and dirt, while a glazed frame tends to obscure the texture of the stitching. Clip frames work well for designs without too much solid detail, but the glass presses on the stitches and flattens them. This type of frame can also allow dirt to penetrate under the glass and this will eventually spoil the fabric. When choosing a conventional picture frame, a window mount will keep the glass from flattening the stitches, or you can use small pieces of wood concealed at each corner of the rebate to lift the glass away from the fabric. After framing, make sure that the gap between frame and mount is sealed with gummed brown paper strip or masking tape to exclude dirt and dust.

SUPPLIERS

Most large department stores carry a good range of fabrics, threads and accessories.
Look in the Yellow Pages for details of your nearest supplier under
'Art and Craft Equipment' or 'Needlecraft Retailers'.

United Kingdom

DMC Creative World Ltd
Head Office
Pullman Road
Wigston
Leicestershire
LE18 2DY
Tel: (0116) 281 1040
DMC threads can be found in
branches of *John Lewis* and
Beatties nationwide.
Phone for your nearest stockist

Craft Creations
Ingersoll House
Delamare Road
Cheshunt
Herts
EN8 9HD
Tel: (01992) 781 900
Website: www.craftcreations.com
Card blanks, tassels, etc.
Mail order only

Creative Beadcraft
Denmark Works
Sheepcote Dell Road
Beamond End, near Amersham
Bucks
HP7 0RX
Tel: (01494) 715 606
Beads
Mail order and stockists

David Morgan Ltd
26 The Hayes
Cardiff
CF1 1UG
Tel: (029) 2022 1011

Delicate Stitches
339 Kentish Town Road
London
NW5 2TJ
Tel: (020) 7267 9403

The Embroidery Shop
51 William Street
Edinburgh
EH3 7LW
Tel: (0131) 225 8642
Fax: (0131) 663 8255
Email:
embroideryshop@gofornet.co.uk

Franklin & Sons
13a-15 St. Botolph's Street
Colchester
CO2 7DU
Tel: (01206) 563955

Fred Aldous
PO Box 135
37 Lever Street
Manchester
M1 1LW
Tel: (0161) 236 2477
Fax: (0161) 236 6075
Mail order craft supplier

Stitches
355 Warwick Road
Olton
Solihull
B91 1BQ
Tel: (0121) 706 1048

Sussex Needlecraft
37 Warwick Street
Worthing
BN11 3DQ
Tel: (01903) 823655

Willow Fabrics
95 Town Lane
Mobberley, Knutsford
Cheshire WA16 7HH
Tel: 0800 056 7811
Website: www.willowfabrics.com
Embroidery fabrics
Mail order only

South Africa

Cape Town Sewing Centre
78 Darling Street
Cape Town
Tel: (021) 465 2111

Johannesburg Sewing Centre
109 Pritchard Street
Johannesburg
Gauteng
Tel: (011) 333 3060

Sew & Save
Mimosa Mall
131 Brandwag
Bloemfontein
Tel: (051) 444 3122

Stitch Craft Centre
5 Umhlanga Centre
Ridge Road
Umhlanga Rocks
Durban
Tel: (031) 561 5822

Stitch Talk
Centurion Park
Centurion Square
Pretoria
Tel: (012) 663 2035

Thimbles & Threads
6 Quarry Centre
Hilton
Pietermaritzburg
Tel: (033) 43 1966

Australia

Barbour Threads Pty Ltd
Suite E3
2 Cowpasture Place
Wetherill Park
NSW 2164
Tel: (02) 9756 5466
Freecall: 1800 337 929

Birch Haberdashery and Craft
EC Birch Pty Ltd
Richmond
Victoria 3121
Tel: (03) 9429 4944

DMC Needlecraft Pty Ltd
51-55 Carrington Road
Marrickville
NSW 2204
Tel: (02) 9559 3088

Lincraft
Gallery Level
Imperial Arcade
Pitt Street
Sydney
NSW 2000
Tel: (02) 9221 5111
Stores nationwide

Sewing Thread Specialists
41-43 Day Street (North)
Silverwater
NSW 2128
Tel: 1300 65 3855

Sullivans Haberdashery and Craft
Wholesalers
40 Parramatta Road
Underwood
Queensland 4119
Tel: (07) 3209 4799

New Zealand

The Embroiderer
140 Hinemoa Street
Birkenhead
Auckland
Tel: (09) 419 0900

Nancy's Embroidery
273 Tinakori Road
Thorndon
Wellington
Tel: (04) 473 4047

Pauline's Needlecraft
94 Clyde Road
Browns Bay
Auckland
Tel: (09) 479 7783

Spotlight Stores
Carry a very large range of fabrics
and haberdashery materials
Manukau - Tel: (09) 263 6760
or 0800 162 373
Wairau Park - Tel: (09) 444 0220
or 0800 224 123
Hamilton - Tel: (07) 839 1793
New Plymouth - Tel: (06) 757 3575
Wellington - Tel: (04) 472 5600
Christchurch - Tel: (03) 377 6121

Stitches
351 Colombo Street
Sydenham
Christchurch
Tel: (03) 379 1868
Email: stitches@xtra.co.nz

For a wider listing of embroidery
suppliers nationwide, consult your
Yellow Pages under 'Handcrafts &
Supplies' or search under 'Shopping:
Hobbies & Games: Handcrafts' on
www.yellowpages.co.nz

INDEX

Page numbers printed in italics refer to photographs